A Practical Guide

to

jBPM5

JBoss Business Process Management Framework

Venkataganesh Thoppae

ISBN: 1492944572
ISBN 13: 9781492944577

Library of Congress Control Number: 2013923209
CreateSpace Independent Publishing Platform
North Charleston, South Carolina

jBPM5
JBOSS BUSINESS PROCESS MANAGEMENT FRAMEWORK

ACKNOWLEDGMENTS

It seems so surreal to me to be authoring a book. When you do something unusual there has to be a reason, and a spark should come from somewhere. For me it came through my friend Udayabaskaran Periyasamy; if not for him, the idea of writing this book would never have originated. Uday happened to see a document I had prepared related to jBPM and suggested that I should write a book on this subject. My first answer was a big, emphatic *no*, without even a second thought. But a day later, out of the blue, a thought suddenly flashed into me: *why not*? I immediately ran this idea by my wife Vani, who after some deliberation encouraged me.

Uday also suggested I launch a crowd-funding project to help with the publishing effort, which again I wouldn't have done if not for him. The crowd-funding project turned out to be an enormous success, and the encouragement shown by family, friends, and community was phenomenal. I am not sure if I would have continued with the book if the crowd-funding project had failed. The confidence showed by the project backers is a big reason I have sustained my enthusiasm.

When I started writing the book, I realized that it is not an easy task, and especially for a debuting author like me. I owe a big thanks to my wife Vani and my wonderful kids Vipula and Vishnu, who put up with me while I was busy at the computer. Vani was so patient with me; if she had charged me a dollar for every coffee she made me in the last few months, she would be a millionaire by now. My kids were so happy that their dad was writing a book but disappointed by the fact that I did not get to spend as much time with them as I used to; they sacrificed a lot more than me. However, they kept me going with their constant words of encouragement.

A couple of well-wishers reviewed the book unofficially and suggested invaluable points. I owe them a big thanks.

In retrospect, this project is a collective team effort: it was started by Uday, funded by crowd-funding project backers, planned and executed by me, and monitored and controlled by reviewers and my family.

Thank you all!

CROWD-FUNDING PROJECT BACKERS

This book was made possible by a group of awesome people who placed tremendous confidence in me and put down their own money so I could write this book, which would not be complete without mentioning their names.

Aaron Anderson
Anil K. Bansal
Tamil Chellaiah
Daniel Gilfrich
Nidhi Gupta
Indyfolks
Karthikeyan Kandasamy
Jeeyun Kim
R. Krishnan
Lakshmi
Manoj Muthukrishnan
Nageswar
Rajendra Singh Narendra
Srihari Padala
Parthasarathy L. Parandapalli
Saravanan Parandapalli
Robert Preller
Amuda S.
G. S. Sankaralingam
Siva Sottallu
Kannan Thoppae
Logan Varatharasa
Srinivasarao Vempati
Annelie Weber

ABOUT THE REVIEWERS

Mariano Nicolas De Maio is the current chief technology officer at Plugtree, working for all of its jBPM and Drools related projects. He graduated from the Universidad Argentina de la Empresa (Enterprise University of Argentina) and has been working with Java-related open-source frameworks for a decade and with Drools and jBPM for the last four years. He has collaborated on many extension points for Drools and jBPM projects integration tools, like Infinispan persistence strategies for Drools, rollbackable process management APIs, and extensions to human task service APIs. He is happily married to Tamara and raising a beautiful baby daughter, Sofia.

Demian Calcaprina is a software engineer, who enjoys new challenges, discovering new ways of doing things and helping others to achieve his goals. Currently he is working as a Drools and jBPM Consultant, encouraging people of using these amazing technologies, and always being active in the community, by writing in the mailing lists, raising tickets and providing bug fixes. He is a happy father, an amateur chess player and a happiness-seeker!

CONTENTS

INTRODUCTION

What Is This Book About?

True to its name, this book is simply a practical guide to jBPM 5.4. It does not explain the theoretical aspects of jBPM and BPMN or build knowledge from the ground up. For instance, it does not explain what a *KnowledgeSession* or what *KnowledgeBuilder* is, or the difference between a *StatefulKnowledgeSession* and a *StatelessKnowledgeSession*. Rather, it illustrates how, when, and where to create a *KnowledgeSession*. Similarly, it does not try to explain all the BPMN2 notations up front and how to represent each and every activity. Instead it explains those notations in the context of a use case, as needed. In summary, this book does not cover each and every single feature provided by jBPM; it covers only very basic and important features. The purpose of this book is to kindle curiosity and lay a basic foundation from which it should be straightforward to explore and learn other features. This book is *not* the bible of jBPM; it is instead a helpful guide that shares some practical nuances.

Why This Book?

jBPM is a great open-source product with a wealth of information available for free. jBPM's source code is available for anyone to download and take a look at. However, much of the information already available is either too involved or too specific to a certain topic. Most of the available resources address different specific features in isolation, but are missing one critical piece—how to put them all together and make them work in a web application. After using jBPM for a while, I sensed an opportunity to fill this gap and help the community with a hands-on book.

Who Is This Book For?

There are two kinds of people that could benefit from this book.

If you are looking for an expedient way to use jBPM in your project or simply looking for a hands-on learning opportunity that does not involve absorbing all the theory first then this book is perfect for you. The first section of the book is aimed at you. It gets you in the trenches right from the start. Without much of effort, you will learn how to start using jBPM.

On the other hand, if you have some experience in jBPM, have looked at its source code, and would like to have some fun by extending or customizing its features, then the second section of the book will be of primary interest to you.

Approach and Tools

This book starts from the premise of building a business workflow for a fictional use case and employing it in a simple JEE application. It uses an iterative methodology in which each step in the business process is built incrementally in each chapter.

Since I am working with a web application, I had to choose from dozens of available frameworks. I initially chose Spring MVC with Spring Managed Transactions and went ahead with about 20 percent of the book. At that point, I realized the extent of digression in the code and possible challenges faced by learners with limited Spring Knowledge. I did not want this to be an impediment for anyone in learning jBPM, which is the sole purpose of this book. So I further simplified the use case/UI components and switched to a good old JSP/Servlet/EJB/JPA model with no third-party framework.

For this book, I assume the reader has a basic understanding and working knowledge of Java, JEE, JBoss, Maven, MySQL (or any RDBMS) and Eclipse.

I used many screenshots in this book because I believe that one picture is worth a thousand words.

Source Code

The source code for the hands-on lessons in this book is available for download. Each chapter has a specific goal and contains step-by-step instructions to realize the goal, while the corresponding source code has the goal already implemented. If there is any hiccup in understanding or following the instructions in the book, the corresponding source code will turn out very handy, especially for section 2, "Advanced Techniques" of the book. The source code can be downloaded in zipped format from Dropbox at http://bit.ly/1bepu5C. The zip file is protected by the password "jbpm5-thoppae".

Conventions

The names of Java classes, methods, variables, files, file locations are italicized, and the on-screen instructions to be followed are in boldface. The code to be copied and the commands to be run from the command line are in a distinct, smaller font and most are in a box. The package names of Java classes are named after a fictitious domain name and the project name where the class resides. For example, *com.bb.bloomrentaldomain.RentalApp* refers to a Java class *RentalApp* in the *bloom-rental-domain* project. Based on this convention, at several places, a fully qualified name of the class is used without referencing its project name.

Feedback

Your comments and feedback are always appreciated. There is a facebook page for this book at https://www.facebook.com/APracticalGuideToJbpm. The author can be reached by messaging in this facebook page; alternatively, you can email him at forjbpm5@brainbloom.net.

SECTION 1
THE BASICS

CHAPTER 1

SETTING THE STAGE

The use case considered for this book is a simple fictitious rental application for apartments.

1.1. Bloom Real Estate: The Rental Application Use Case

Bloom Real Estate owns several apartment buildings across North America, each with an administrative and management office. Currently, potential renters must walk into a Bloom office, fill out a paper application form, and hand it in to the office manager. The candidates' creditworthiness is manually assessed, along with several other things, and their eligibility is determined. Everything works fine, except that this process is laborious, sometimes resulting in a severe backlog of applications. Besides, this does not offer much flexibility to the applicants or the assessing office manager. Several applicants have inquired if there is a way to submit the application electronically. Therefore, management has decided to make the application available on the Bloom Real Estate website and automate the rental application process. After several rounds of serious discussions, management came up with a simple flow diagram representing the process. The flow diagram is shown below.

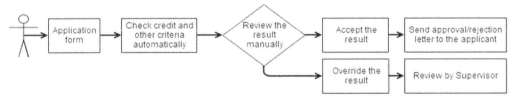

Figure 1. The rental application flow diagram.

- Candidates fill out and submit the application form at the website.

- An automated process determines applicants' eligibility based on credit score and other factors.

- An office manager manually verifies the result of the automated process and either accepts or overrides the result.

- If the result is accepted as is, a letter is sent to the applicant to indicate the approval or rejection.

- If the officer overrides the result, a supervisor reviews the process and then a letter is sent to the applicant.

The rest of this book details implementing this business process using jBPM. Since the definition of a business process in jBPM is stored in an XML format according to BPMN2 specification, hereafter a business process is referred to as BPM or alternatively as a BPMN2 process.

1.1.1. Setting Up the Environment

As has been noted in the official jBPM user guide, the easiest way to set up a jBPM environment is by using the jBPM full installer, which uses an *ant* build script to pull all required resources from the Internet. The script can also be tweaked to suit your exact needs. Since we may not need everything from the installer, we will handpick a few things and install them manually here.

1.1.2. Installing Web Designer

The recommended editor for creating a jBPM business process is a web-based designer that uses *Drools Guvnor* as a storage repository for publishing knowledge assets like business processes and related assets like rule files, images, work item definition files, domain JAR files, and the like. Applications can also directly consume the resources from *Guvnor* Repository in runtime. In order to focus solely on jBPM without worrying about the nitty-gritty of Guvnor, once a resource is created in the designer, we will grab it and put it inside the application code base, so the application will have no dependency of *Guvnor* in runtime. *Web Designer* itself is a web application, and so is *Drools Guvnor*, the storage repository. The first step is getting *Web Designer* up and running, for which we need to download WAR files for both *Web Designer* and *Guvnor*.

- Install Java 1.6 (update 45). The JAVA_HOME environment variable should point to the JDK location.

- Install JBoss AS 7.1.1. For the remainder of this book, $JBOSS_HOME will refer to the root location of the JBoss installation directory.

- Download the *jbpm-designer-2.4.0.Final-jboss7.war* file for process designer from http://sourceforge.net/projects/jbpm/files/designer/. Rename the WAR file as *designer.war*.

Figure 2. Downloading Web Designer.

- Download *guvnor-distribution-5.5.0.Final.zip* from http://www.jboss.org/drools/downloads. The current version is greater than 5.5; scroll down at the above link to find the download for version 5.5. Extract and grab the file *guvnor-5.5.0.Final-jboss-as-7.0.war* from the binaries folder. Rename this file as *drools-guvnor.war*.

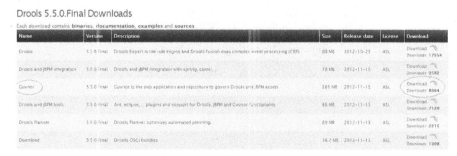

Figure 3. Downloading Drools Guvnor.

- Drop the above two WAR files into *$JBOSS_HOME/standalone/deployments*. Go to JBOSS_HOME and bring up the server from there by running either *.\bin\standalone. sh* or *.\bin\standalone.bat*, depending on your operating system; http://localhost:8080/drools-guvnor should bring up *Guvnor* Repository.

- When you access *Guvnor* for the first time, it will prompt to install a sample repository as shown below; choose "No, Thanks" for that option. (It could take a good ten or fifteen seconds for this pop-up dialog to appear. In case your installation doesn't prompt you, don't fret; keep moving, as we are not going to use that repository in this guide anyway).

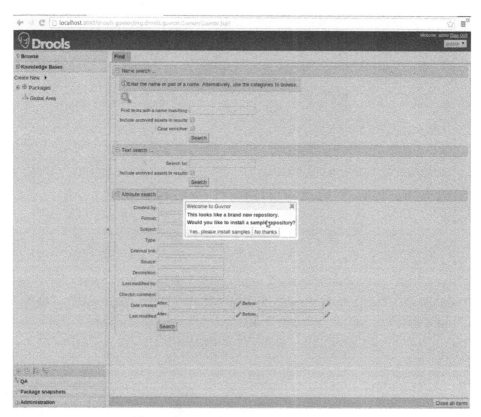

Figure 4. Installing a sample repository.

ALERT:

Windows Only: If the designer deployment times out, increase the timeout by adding *deployment-timeout in $JBOSS_HOME/standalone/configuration/standalone.xml:*

```
<subsystem xmlns="urn:jboss:domain:deployment-scanner:1.1">
<deployment-scanner path="deployments" relative-to="jboss.server.base.
dir"
    scan-interval="5000" deployment-timeout="600"/>
</subsystem>
```

1.1.3. Setting Up the Project Structure

Next let us set up our project structure, which will give placeholders to create files and resources where necessary. The project is a typical JEE application with four different modules: Domain, Web, EJB, and EAR. We will be using Maven to compile and manage the dependencies. The root/parent project is called *bloom-rental* with four different modules called *bloom-rental-ear*, *bloom-rental-domain*, *bloom-rental-web*, and *bloom-rental-ejb*.

- Download Maven 3.1.1 from http://maven.apache.org/download.cgi and install following the installation instructions from the same page. Make sure `mvn -version` works fine from the command line, showing installed Maven and Java version. (If your system has a different version of Maven, you can continue to use the same; it should not cause a problem).

- Install *Eclipse IDE* for Java Developers (*Version: 4.3.1—Kepler*) from http://www.eclipse.org/downloads/.

- Open Eclipse and create a workspace called *bloom-workspace*.

- Create a directory called *bloom-rental* under *bloom-workspace*.

- In your favorite editor, create a file called *pom.xml* at *bloom-rental* with the contents below to start with. This will be the parent POM for all modules.

```xml
<?xml version="1.0" encoding="UTF-8"?>
<project xmlns="http://maven.apache.org/POM/4.0.0"xmlns:xsi="http://
www.w3.org/2001/XMLSchema-instance"xsi:schemalocation="http://maven.
apache.org/POM/4.0.0 http://maven.apache.org/mavenv4_0_0.xsd ">
<modelVersion>4.0.0</modelVersion>
<groupId>com.bb</groupId>
<artifactId>bloom-rental</artifactId>
<packaging>pom</packaging>
<version>1.0.0</version>
<name>bloom-rental</name>
<properties>
    <project.build.sourceEncoding>UTF-8</project.build.sourceEncoding>
</properties>
<modules>
</modules>
<build>
<plugins>
  <plugin>
      <groupId>org.apache.maven.plugins</groupId>
      <artifactId>maven-compiler-plugin</artifactId>
      <version>2.3.2</version>
      <configuration>
      <source>1.6</source>
      <target>1.6</target>
  </configuration>
</plugin>
</plugins>
  </build>
</project>
```

- To create individual modules, run the commands below in a command line separately, one after another, from *bloom-rental* directory. The differences in each command are in bold.

```
  mvn archetype:generate -DarchetypeArtifactId=maven-archetype-
quickstart -DgroupId=com.bb -DartifactId=bloom-rental-domain
-DinteractiveMode=false
```

```
mvn archetype:generate -DarchetypeGroupId=org.codehaus.mojo.arche-
types -DarchetypeArtifactId=webapp-javaee6 -DinteractiveMode=false
-DgroupId=com.bb -DartifactId=bloom-rental-web
```

```
mvn archetype:generate -DarchetypeGroupId=org.codehaus.mojo.arche-
types -DarchetypeArtifactId=ejb-javaee6 -DinteractiveMode=false
-DgroupId=com.bb -DartifactId=bloom-rental-ejb
```

```
mvn archetype:generate -DarchetypeGroupId=org.codehaus.mojo.arche-
types -DarchetypeArtifactId=ear-javaee6 -DinteractiveMode=false
-DgroupId=com.bb -DartifactId=bloom-rental-ear
```

This creates a project each for the Domain, Web, EJB, and EAR modules, updating the
<modules> section of *bloom-rental/pom.xml* during the process.

- From *bloom-workspace* in Eclipse, select **File->Import->Maven->Existing Maven Projects** and click **Next**.

- Select *bloom-rental*, click **Next** and **Finish** to import all POM files.

ALERT:

Depending on the m2e plugin version in Eclipse, during import, maven-dependency-plugin might report an error followed by a warning for "Incomplete Maven Goal Execution" when you finish the import wizard. If so, after import, Markers/Problems view might display a "Maven Problem" under Markers/Problems view that looks like this:

Plugin execution not covered by lifecycle configuration: org.apache.maven.plugins:maven-dependency-plugin:2.1:copy (execution: default, phase: validate)

This is a long-standing issue with the m2e plugin. You can make m2e happy by following these steps:

- Select the error; right click and select Quick Fix. Select Permanently mark goal copy in pom.xml as ignored in Eclipse build and select Finish.

- There will be a pop-up box to identify the location where the fix is to be placed. Select bloom-rental and click OK.

- From the Project Explorer, select bloom-rental project and right click->Maven->Update Project and click OK. The errors should be gone.

- Remove <groupId> from the *pom.xml* of all the modules except the parent POM to make other warnings go away.

- Make the following changes in *bloom-rental-ear/pom.xml*.

  - Add *bloom-rental-web, bloom-rental-ejb*, and *bloom-rental-domain* as dependencies.

```xml
<dependencies>
    <dependency>
        <groupId>com.bb</groupId>
        <artifactId>bloom-rental-web</artifactId>
        <version>1.0-SNAPSHOT</version>
        <type>war</type>
    </dependency>
    <dependency>
            <groupId>com.bb</groupId>
            <artifactId>bloom-rental-ejb</artifactId>
            <version>1.0-SNAPSHOT</version>
            <type>ejb</type>
    </dependency>
    <dependency>
            <groupId>com.bb</groupId>
            <artifactId>bloom-rental-domain</artifactId>
            <version>1.0-SNAPSHOT</version>
            <type>jar</type>
    </dependency>
</dependencies>
```

- Add *bloom-rental-web* and *bloom-rental-ejb* as modules under *maven-ear-plugin*. Only the section in bold needs to be copied in the appropriate place.

```xml
<plugin>
  <groupId>org.apache.maven.plugins</groupId>
  <artifactId>maven-ear-plugin</artifactId>
  <version>2.6</version>
  <configuration>
    <version>6</version>
    <defaultLibBundleDir>lib</defaultLibBundleDir>
    <modules>
     <webModule>
       <groupId>com.bb</groupId>
       <artifactId>bloom-rental-web</artifactId>
       <bundleFileName>bloom-rental-web-1.0-
SNAPSHOT.war</bundleFileName>
       <contextRoot>/bloom-rental</contextRoot>
     </webModule>
     <ejbModule>
       <groupId>com.bb</groupId>
       <artifactId>bloom-rental-ejb</artifactId>
       <bundleFileName>bloom-rental-ejb-1.0-
SNAPSHOT.jar</bundleFileName>
     </ejbModule>
    </modules>
  </configuration>
</plugin>
```

- Add *bloom-rental-domain* as a dependency in both *bloom-rental-web* and *bloom-rental-ejb* POM files.

```
<dependency>
    <groupId>com.bb</groupId>
    <artifactId>bloom-rental-domain</artifactId>
    <version>1.0-SNAPSHOT</version>
    <type>jar</type>
</dependency>
```

- Add *bloom-rental-ejb* as a dependency in the *bloom-rental-web* POM file.

```
<dependency>
        <groupId>com.bb</groupId>
        <artifactId>bloom-rental-ejb</artifactId>
        <version>1.0-SNAPSHOT</version>
        <type>jar</type>
</dependency>
```

- Select the **bloom-rental** project, **right click->Maven->Update Project->OK**.

- Create *application.xml* under *bloom-rental-ear/src/main/application/META-INF*, and add the following contents.

```xml
<?xml version="1.0" encoding="UTF-8"?>
<application xmlns="http://java.sun.com/xml/ns/javaee"xmlns:xsi="http://
www.w3.org/2001/XMLSchema-instance"xsi:schemaLocation="http://java.
sun.com/xml/ns/javaee http://java.sun.com/xml/ns/javaee/application_6.
xsd"version="6">
    <display-name>bloom-rental-ear</display-name>
    <module>
     <web>
       <web-uri>bloom-rental-web-1.0-SNAPSHOT.war</web-uri>
       <context-root>/bloom-rental</context-root>
     </web>
    </module>
    <module>
     <ejb>bloom-rental-ejb-1.0-SNAPSHOT.jar</ejb>
    </module>
    <library-directory>lib</library-directory>
    </application>
```

- In *MANIFEST.MF* of *bloom-rental-ear* project, add the `Dependencies` as below and make sure there is a new line at the end.

```
Manifest-Version: 1.0
Dependencies: org.dom4j export
```

- To get rid of unwanted warnings related to JPA/JSP in Eclipse, turn off build time validation for JPA and JSP from **Window->Preferences->Validation** as indicated below.

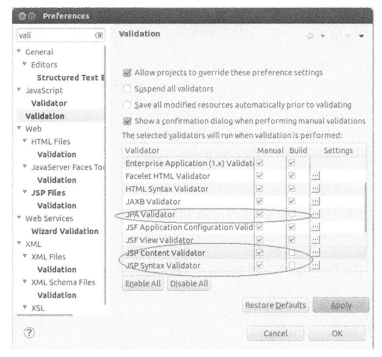

Figure 5. Turning off JPA-JSP validation.

- From the command prompt at *bloom-rental*, do an `mvn install` to generate the target *bloom-rental-ear-1.0-SNAPSHOT.ear*.

- Deploy the target file (*bloom-rental-ear-1.0-SNAPSHOT.ear*) by manually copying it from *bloom-rental/bloom-rental-ear/target* to *$JBOSS_HOME/standalone/deployments*.

- Go to the browser and enter http://localhost:8080/bloom-rental. A "Hello World" banner should welcome you.

1.1.4. Setting Up jBPM Binaries

Manually downloading jBPM binaries and all their dependencies can be a hassle. Maven handily automates this process. Simply add all jBPM dependencies in pom.xml, which will automate their download during the first Maven life cycle operation. Since jBPM interactions are going to be restricted only in the EJB layer, make the following changes only in *bloom-rental-ejb/pom.xml*.

- Add a property of `<jbpm.version>5.4.0.Final</jbpm.version>`.

- Add the following dependencies

```
<dependency>
        <groupId>dom4j</groupId>
        <artifactId>dom4j</artifactId>
        <version>1.6.1</version>
        <scope>provided</scope>
</dependency>
<dependency>
        <groupId>org.hibernate</groupId>
        <artifactId>hibernate-core</artifactId>
        <version>3.3.2.GA</version>
        <scope>test</scope>
</dependency>
<dependency>
        <groupId>org.hibernate</groupId>
        <artifactId>hibernate-entitymanager</artifactId>
        <version>3.4.0.GA</version>
        <scope>test</scope>
</dependency>
<dependency>
        <groupId>org.jbpm</groupId>
        <artifactId>jbpm-flow</artifactId>
        <version>${jbpm.version}</version>
</dependency>
<dependency>
        <groupId>org.jbpm</groupId>
        <artifactId>jbpm-flow-builder</artifactId>
        <version>${jbpm.version}</version>
</dependency>
<dependency>
        <groupId>org.jbpm</groupId>
        <artifactId>jbpm-bpmn2</artifactId>
        <version>${jbpm.version}</version>
</dependency>
```

```
<dependency>
        <groupId>org.jbpm</groupId>
        <artifactId>jbpm-human-task-core</artifactId>
        <version>${jbpm.version}</version>
</dependency>
<dependency>
        <groupId>org.jbpm</groupId>
        <artifactId>jbpm-persistence-jpa</artifactId>
        <version>${jbpm.version}</version>
</dependency>
<dependency>
        <groupId>org.jbpm</groupId>
        <artifactId>jbpm-bam</artifactId>
        <version>${jbpm.version}</version>
</dependency>
<dependency>
        <groupId>commons-dbcp</groupId>
        <artifactId>commons-dbcp</artifactId>
        <version>1.4</version>
</dependency>
<dependency>
        <groupId>org.slf4j</groupId>
        <artifactId>slf4j-api</artifactId>
        <version>1.5.6</version>
</dependency>
<dependency>
        <groupId>org.slf4j</groupId>
        <artifactId>jcl-over-slf4j</artifactId>
        <version>1.5.6</version>
</dependency>
<dependency>
        <groupId>org.slf4j</groupId>
        <artifactId>slf4j-log4j12</artifactId>
<version>1.5.6</version>
</dependency>
```

- From *bloom-rental* project, **right click->Maven->Update Project->OK**.

- Go to *bloom-rental* in Terminal/Command Prompt and do an `mvn clean install`. This will pull down all the jBPM binaries and their dependencies from the Maven repository.

- Deploy the EAR target again; go to the browser and check that the URL http://localhost:8080/bloom-rental displays "Hello World," as earlier.

1.1.5. Setting Up the Database

For each jBPM process there is an underlying **process instance** object that is hosted by a **session instance** object. These objects and several other related objects can either be persistent or nonpersistent. If a process is a long-running one, then it can take days or weeks to complete; a nonpersistent process in memory simply does not make sense for such cases. Therefore, in this book we will use a persistent mechanism to store jBPM sessions and processes. This guide uses the MySQL database for persisting model data.

- Install Version 5.5.34 of MySQL Community Server from http://dev.mysql.com/downloads/mysql/5.5.html#downloads. The reason for using a lower version of MySQL will be explained in chapter 5.

- Start it up, and create a database named *bloomdb*. Write down the user ID and password for the database server.

1.1.6. Setting Up the Data Source

The JBoss application server should be provided access to the database with a data source. If it is the first time your JBoss instance is using MySQL, you need to follow all of the steps below; otherwise you can go straight to making changes in *standalone.xml*.

- Download MySQL connnector/J: *mysql-connector-java-5.1.27*, distributed from http://dev.mysql.com/downloads/connector/j/#download. Extract and grab the *mysql-connector-java-5.1.27-bin.jar* file.

- Create a folder *com/mysql/main* under *$JBOSS_HOME/modules*, and drop the Mysql connector JAR file under *com/mysql/main*.

- Create a *module.xml* file under *com/mysql/main* to identify the location of the JAR file and copy the below contents in that file.

```xml
<?xml version="1.0" encoding="UTF-8"?>
<module xmlns="urn:jboss:module:1.1" name="com.mysql">
    <resources>
        <resource-root path="mysql-connector-java-5.1.27-bin.jar"/>
    </resources>
    <dependencies>
        <module name="javax.api" />
    </dependencies>
</module>
```

- Open the *$JBOSS_HOME/standalone/configuration/standalone.xml* file.

- Look for the `<datasource>` section, and add an entry for our data source as shown below. Replace **XXX** with your username and password for the MySQL database instance.

```
<datasource jndi-name="java:jboss/datasources/bloomDS" pool-
name="bloomDS" enabled="true" use-java-context="true">
        <connection-url>jdbc:mysql://localhost:3306/bloomdb</
        connection-url>
        <driver>mysql</driver>
        <security>
                <user-name>XXX</user-name>
                <password>XXX</password>
        </security>
</datasource>
```

- Add the following under <drivers>.

```
<driver name="mysql" module="com.mysql">
    <xa-datasource-class>
      com.mysql.jdbc.jdbc2.optional.MysqlXADataSource
    </xa-datasource-class>
</driver>
```

The data source is all set to use now. Restart the JBOSS server so the changes made are picked up and the data source is bound to JNDI.

Summary

We have taken slow but steady steps to successfully set up an environment with jBPM Web Designer, a JEE project structure pointing to a Maven repository with all jBPM dependencies, a MySQL database, and an application server configured to use that database and ready to host a jBPM application.

CHAPTER 2:

THE HELLO WORLD BPM

When we are hungry and have a meal in front of us, we should devour it. So now that we have an environment, let's get our hands dirty with a simple Hello World BPM. Our modus operandi in this chapter and for the remainder of the book is always as follows:

- Design a BPM process in the designer.

- Generate an image, validate, save, and check in.

- Export the BPMN file and copy it in the Eclipse workspace.

- Complete the application-related code changes.

- Do a Maven build with `mvn clean install`.

- Deploy the target EAR in JBoss.

- Test the application.

2.1. Designing the Hello World Process

As was noted in chapter 1, *Web Designer* helps to design the BPMN2 process and, by default, stores the designed process in *Guvnor* Repository. Applications using BPMN2 process have a choice of using the process in the repository or keeping process files locally along with the EAR/WAR file. While it is always recommended to directly consume process from the *Guvnor* repository, just to keep it simple and not to deviate from our focus on jBPM, in this book we will be following the local storage mechanism.

- Make sure the JBoss server is running. Access the designer using the URL http://localhost:8080/drools-guvnor.

- Click on **Knowledge Bases**.

- Select **Create New -> New Package**.

- Leave the default selection of **Create new package**. Give the new package name as *com.bb* and click **Create package**.

- Select **Create New -> New BPMN2 Process**.

- Give the process name as *helloworld*; leave the package as *com.bb* and click **OK**.

Figure 6. Creating a new process.

- You should get a screen like the one below; click on the >> icon (circled in the picture below) to see the shapes palette.

Figure 7. Clicking to show the icons palette.

• Switch to the **jBPM BPMN2 (Minimal)** perspective; the features offered by this perspective should be enough for most uses.

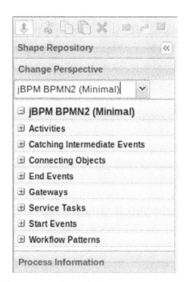

Figure 8. The Minimal perspective.

• The process needs a start event to get started. So expand **Start Events** from the left and select **Start Event**; drag and drop it to the canvas.

• Once the process is started, all we want to do is print "Hello World'" in the console. We will be using a task node to do that job. Select on the green Start Event in the canvas, which will bring a context-sensitive palette as shown below. Click on the square shaped icon for the task. It will place a task node on the canvas and automatically draw a connector (sequence) from the *Start Event* to the task node.

Figure 9. The context-sensitive palette.

• BPMN2 supports different types of tasks. The one we just put on the canvas is an abstract task; as such it is not enough. We need to tell it what the exact type of this task is. To do that, click on the tool icon on the bottom-left edge of the task; it will pull down a menu with all supported task types. For our purpose now, select the one that reads *Script Task*. A script task is something that will execute a script upon invocation.

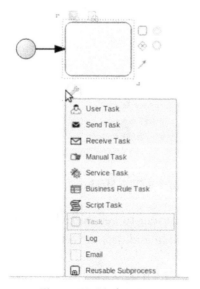

Figure 10. Task types.

- Click on the << icon (circled in the picture below) at the right edge of the canvas to bring up the Properties pane.

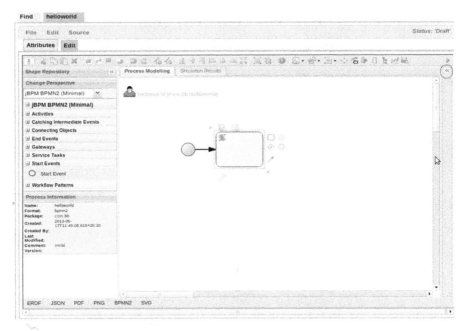

Figure 11. Clicking to show the properties pane.

- Selecting an empty area on the canvas will show the properties of the process in the Properties pane. Expand the **Extra** Section in the Properties pane. Note the ID of the process, which is by default *<package name>.<process name>*. It becomes in this case *com.bb.helloworld*. This will be the identifier for the process for any program to make a reference to it. The process has to be started using this ID.

Figure 12. The process properties.

- Now select the *Script Task* on the canvas and expand the **Extra** section in the Properties pane. Click on the drop-down menu for the property **Script**, which should bring an Expression Editor.

- Type the following, and click on **OK** to exit the expression editor.

```
System.out.println("Hello World");
```

- Under the **Common** section in the Properties pane, name the script task *Hello World*.

- An end event is needed to gracefully end the process. Select *Script Task* and select the circle with the thick single border from the context-sensitive palette, which is the end event.

- Click on the PNG tab below the canvas to generate the image for the process and download it. Depending on your browser setting, it may prompt for the location to download the image. Select a location and remember it.

- Now the top section of the canvas will show a series of icons. Look for the Validate process icon  toward the right side. Click that icon to validate the process, which should report no validation errors.

- At this time save the process and check it in by selecting **File->Save Changes**.

- Your process should like this:

Figure 13. The Hello World process.

2.2. Exporting the Process to the Eclipse Workspace

The *Web Designer* has helped to create a process per BPMN2 specification. Now we need to take this process and put it into the application workspace, where it will live with its friends and family, the rest of the code base.

- Click on the **BPMN2** tab at the bottom of the canvas; it will show the BPMN2 source of the process.

- Click **Save to File**; the browser will download a file named *com.bb.helloworld.bpmn2* to the file system, either at a default location or via a prompt to choose a location.

2.3. Updating the Application

Now that we have a BPMN file, the next step is to invoke it from a web application. In order to do that, we are going to build on the *bloom-rental* JEE app created earlier. Our strategy would be to always work backward: start from the back end and finish with the front end. Let us make a few changes in the *bloom-rental-ejb* and *bloom-rental-web* projects as noted below.

<u>bloom-rental-ejb</u>

- Copy the BPMN file *com.bb.helloworld.bpmn2* downloaded from the *Guvnor* in the previous section to the directory *src/main/resources*.

- Create *persistence.xml* under *src/main/resources/META-INF* and copy the following contents.

```xml
<?xml version="1.0" encoding="UTF-8" standalone="yes"?>
    <persistence version="1.0" xsi:schemaLocation= "http://java.sun.com/
    xml/ns/persistence
        http://java.sun.com/xml/ns/persistence/persistence_1_0.xsd
        http://java.sun.com/xml/ns/persistence/orm
        http://java.sun.com/xml/ns/persistence/orm_1_0.xsd"
    xmlns:orm="http://java.sun.com/xml/ns/persistence/orm"
    xmlns:xsi="http://www.w3.org/2001/XMLSchema-instance"
    xmlns="http://java.sun.com/xml/ns/persistence">
        <persistence-unit name="jpa.jbpm" transaction-type="JTA">
        <provider>org.hibernate.ejb.HibernatePersistence</provider>
        <jta-data-source>java:jboss/datasources/bloomDS</jta-data-source>
        <mapping-file>META-INF/JBPMorm.xml</mapping-file>
        <mapping-file>META-INF/ProcessInstanceInfo.hbm.xml</mapping-file>
        <class>org.drools.persistence.info.SessionInfo</class>
    <class>org.jbpm.persistence.processinstance.ProcessInstanceInfo</
    class>
        <class>org.drools.persistence.info.WorkItemInfo</class>
        <properties>
          <property name="hibernate.dialect" value="org.hibernate.dia-
          lect.MySQLDialect"/>
          <property name="hibernate.max_fetch_depth" value="3"/>
          <property name="hibernate.hbm2ddl.auto" value="update"/>
          <property name="hibernate.show_sql" value="true"/>
          <property name="hibernate.transaction.manag-
          er_lookup_class" value="org.hibernate.transaction.
          JBossTransactionManagerLookup"/>
          <property name="hibernate.connection.driver_class"
                    value="com.mysql.jdbc.Driver"/>
      </properties>
    </persistence-unit>
</persistence>
```

This *persistence.xml* defines a persistence unit called *jpa.jbpm*, which uses *Hibernate* as the JPA provider and MySQL as the database. The mapping files *JBPMorm.xml* and *ProcessInstanceInfo.hbm.xml* are packaged with the jBPM binaries.

- Create a stateless EJB *com.bb.bloomrentalejb.process.ProcessFacade* with a local interface *com.bb.bloomrentalejb.process.ProcessFacadeLocal* and define a method called *startProcess()* in the interface with the signature below. This method will be the one kicking off the business process based on the given process ID.

```
public void startProcess(String processId);
```

- Declare at the top of ProcessFacade EJB that it uses Bean Managed Transaction.

```
@Stateless
@TransactionManagement(TransactionManagementType.BEAN)
public class ProcessFacade implements ProcessFacadeLocal {
```

- Inject an instance of EntityManagerFactory.

```
@PersistenceUnit(unitName = "jpa.jbpm")
private EntityManagerFactory emf;
```

- Implement the startProcess () method in ProcessFacade EJB as shown below. I will go over some important points here.

```
package com.bb.bloomrentalejb.process;
import javax.ejb.Stateless;
import javax.ejb.TransactionManagement;
import javax.ejb.TransactionManagementType;
import javax.naming.Context;
import javax.naming.InitialContext;
import javax.persistence.EntityManagerFactory;
import javax.persistence.PersistenceUnit;
import javax.transaction.UserTransaction;
import org.drools.KnowledgeBase;
import org.drools.KnowledgeBaseFactory;
import org.drools.builder.KnowledgeBuilder;
import org.drools.builder.KnowledgeBuilderFactory;
import org.drools.builder.ResourceType;
import org.drools.io.ResourceFactory;
import org.drools.persistence.jpa.JPAKnowledgeService;
import org.drools.runtime.Environment;
import org.drools.runtime.EnvironmentName;
import org.drools.runtime.StatefulKnowledgeSession;
@Stateless
@TransactionManagement(TransactionManagementType.BEAN)
public class ProcessFacade implements ProcessFacadeLocal {
    @PersistenceUnit(unitName = "jpa.jbpm")
    private EntityManagerFactory emf;
@Override
    public void startProcess(String processId) {
        System.out.println("startProcess called");
        System.out.println("Running process for" + processId);
        startBPM(processId);
        System.out.println("Process successfully started...");
    }
```

```
public void startBPM(String processId) {
        UserTransaction ut = null;
        StatefulKnowledgeSession ksession = null;
        try {
        Context ctx = new InitialContext();
        ut = (UserTransaction) ctx.lookup("java:comp/UserTransaction");
        ut.begin();

KnowledgeBuilder kbuilder = KnowledgeBuilderFactory
                                                .newKnowledgeBuilder();
kbuilder.add(
        ResourceFactory.newClassPathResource("com.bb.helloworld.bpmn2"),
        ResourceType.BPMN2);    KnowledgeBase kbase = kbuilder.
        newKnowledgeBase();
ksession = JPAKnowledgeService.newStatefulKnowledgeSession(kbase,
                                        null, createEnvironment());
ksession.startProcess(processId, null);
ut.commit();
} catch (Exception e) {
    e.printStackTrace();
    try {
    ut.rollback();
    } catch (Exception ex) {
    ex.printStackTrace();
    }
} finally {
    try {
       ksession.dispose();
       } catch (Exception ex) {
       ex.printStackTrace();
       }
       } }
       private Environment createEnvironment() {
    Environment environment = KnowledgeBaseFactory.newEnvironment();
    environment.set(EnvironmentName.ENTITY_MANAGER_FACTORY, emf);
    return environment;
}
}
```

First a transactional context is initiated: creating a default knowledge builder, adding the BPM processes to the knowledge builder, and creating a knowledge base from the builder. Then *JPAKnowledgeService* is used to create a stateful knowledge session (referred to as a *ksession*) based on the knowledge base just created and also providing a new environment context with it, which is created in a separate method.

The environment object basically identifies the caller environment to jBPM context and provides a reference to it by means of an EntityManagerFactory reference, which will of course be used by jBPM internally to create EntityManager.

The knowledge session is used to start the process identified by the given ID, which should be the value of the ID property of the jBPM process.

bloom-rental-web

- Create a POJO called *com.bb.bloomrentalweb.processor.AppProcessor* to look up the *ProcessFacade* EJB and call its *startProcess()* method.

```
package com.bb.bloomrentalweb.processor;
import javax.naming.Context;
import javax.naming.InitialContext;
import com.bb.bloomrentalejb.process.ProcessFacadeLocal;
public class AppProcessor {
    public void processApp()
    {
        try {
            Context context = new InitialContext();
            ProcessFacadeLocal processFacade =
            (ProcessFacadeLocal)
    context.lookup("java:module/ProcessFacade");
            processFacade.startProcess("com.bb.helloworld");
        } catch (Exception e) {
            e.printStackTrace();
        }
    }
}
```

- Now we need a front-end UI from which the user can initiate the Hello World process. Create a directory *WEB-INF/views* under *src/main/webapp* and create a JSP page called *app.jsp* under *WEB-INF/views*; define just a form with a Submit button on the JSP page as noted below.

```
<%@page contentType="text/html" pageEncoding="UTF-8"%>
<!DOCTYPE HTML PUBLIC "-//W3C//DTD HTML 4.01 Transitional//EN"
        "http://www.w3.org/TR/html4/loose.dtd">
<html>
<head>
<meta http-equiv="Content-Type" content="text/html; charset=UTF-8">
<title>Bloom Apartments</title>
</head>
<body>
        <h2>Rental Application - Hello World</h2>
        <form action="submitapp" method="POST">
                <table border="none">
                <tr>
                <td colspan="2"><input type="SUBMIT" value="Start BPM"
                /></td>
                </tr>
                </table>
        </form>
</body>
</html>
```

- Create a servlet *com.bb.bloomrentalweb.controller.AppServlet* to show *app.jsp* as well as to handle the submission request from this JSP. This servlet will function as a front controller, be a lightweight, without any actual processing logic. It delegates the request to AppProcessor.

```
package com.bb.bloomrentalweb.controller;
import java.io.IOException;
import javax.servlet.RequestDispatcher;
import javax.servlet.ServletException;
import javax.servlet.annotation.WebServlet;
import javax.servlet.http.HttpServlet;
import javax.servlet.http.HttpServletRequest;
import javax.servlet.http.HttpServletResponse;
import com.bb.bloomrentalweb.processor.AppProcessor;
@WebServlet(name="/AppServlet", urlPatterns= {"/showapp", "/submitapp"})
public class AppServlet extends HttpServlet {
        private static final long serialVersionUID = 1L;
        protected void doGet(HttpServletRequest request,
        HttpServletResponse response) throws ServletException,
        IOException {
                this.doPost(request, response);
        }
        protected void doPost(HttpServletRequest request,
        HttpServletResponse response) throws ServletException,
        IOException {
        if (request.getRequestURI().contains("showapp")) {
            showApp(request, response);
        } else if (request.getRequestURI().contains("submitapp")) {
            processApp(request, response);
         }
        }
        public void showApp(HttpServletRequest request,
        HttpServletResponse response) throws ServletException,
        IOException {
        RequestDispatcher disp= request.getRequestDispatcher("WEB-INF/
        views/app.jsp");
        disp.forward(request, response);
        }
        public void processApp(HttpServletRequest request,
        HttpServletResponse response) throws ServletException,
        IOException{
        AppProcessor processor = new AppProcessor();
        processor.processApp();
        response.sendRedirect("showapp");
        }
}
```

2.4. Running the Application

Now we have all the infrastructure ready to run the Hello World BPM. Do an `mvn in-stall` from *bloom-workspace\bloom-rental* directory in the command line and deploy the EAR file in JBOSS; http://localhost:8080/bloom-rental/showapp should display the *app.jsp* page. Click on the **Start BPM** button to submit the page. This should trigger the business process and print "Hello World" in the console.

Summary

In chapter 1 we set up an environment with a JEE project, Maven repository, application server, and database. We have taken a crucial step forward in this chapter to learn to create and run a simple Hello World jBPM process by connecting all the dots. This entailed many things; one of them was using *Web Designer*. I encourage you to play around with *Web Designer* and *Guvnor* to explore their features and capabilities.

CHAPTER 3

THE BLOOM RENTAL APPLICATION: ADDING A SERVICE TASK

We have a decent start so far by creating and running a simple BPM process; now it is time to dive into the Bloom rental application use case that we talked about in chapter 1. As was noted in the introduction, we are going to develop this use case incrementally, one node at a time. Referring back to figure 1, when an application is submitted to Bloom Real Estate, the first thing to happen is the determination of the applicant's credit score. Typically the credit score is obtained by using some third-party API. In our case, for the sake of simplicity, we will simply generate a random score between 500 and 800 and pretend that is the credit score. We will write a Java code to generate a random credit score and call up this code from BPM using what is called a *Service Task*, which—as its name implies—is simply used to invoke a service.

3.1. Designing the Process

- Following the steps for the *Hello World* process, create a new BPMN2 process, *bloom-rentalapp*, under the package *com.bb* and switch to the Minimal perspective.

- From the Properties pane, note that the ID of the process is *com.bb.bloomrentalapp* and its name is set to *bloomrentalapp*.

- Add *Start Event* and select it to bring the context-sensitive palette.

- Select the square icon from the context-sensitive palette to drop a task node into the canvas.

- Select the tool icon under the bottom left edge of the task node to pull up the list of tasks; select *Service Task* in that. Now the task node will show two gears at the top left corner to indicate that it is a service task. Name the service task *Credit Service Task* from the properties pane.

- With the service task selected, select the small circle icon from the context-sensitive palette to bring up the end event node on the canvas. The process should look like this:

Figure 14. The Bloom rental application with a service task.

- Within the properties of the process, under **Extra** section, click on the arrow at **Variable Definitions** to bring up a dialog box. Click on **Add Variable**, create an entry as indicated below, and click **OK**. This variable app will act as a data carrier between the process and the program calling it. We are declaring that the app is of custom type *com.bb.bloomrentaldomain.RentalApp*, which will be defined in the *bloom-rental-domain* project later.

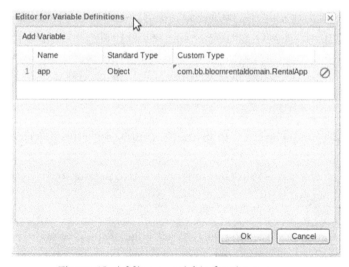

Figure 15. Adding a variable for the process.

- The above step has defined a process variable, but we still need to define a local variable for the *Credit Service Task*. Select *Credit Service Task* and bring its properties pane. Click on the arrow at **DataInputSet** under **Extra**; click on **Add Data Input** and define a local variable as shown below. Because of the way the default service task handler is coded, all service task input variables must be named *Parameter* with *Object* as type. Click **OK**.

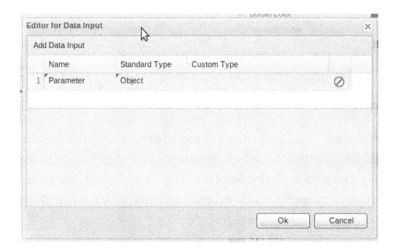

Figure 16. Adding a variable for the service task.

- Now we have a process-level variable and a local variable for the service task. In order for the service task context to have complete access to the process variable, we should pass the data from the process scope to the service task. With *Credit Service Task* selected, click on the drop-down arrow at **Assignments** and define the mapping by clicking on **Add Assignment** as indicated below.

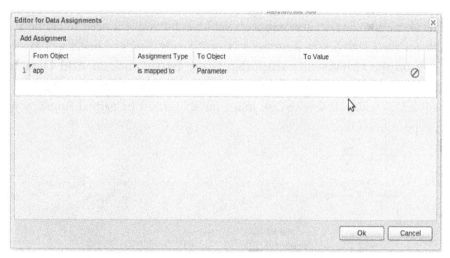

Figure 17. Data assignment for the credit service task.

- The service task is all about executing a method in a Java class. So let's define the Java class and method that is to be executed for this service task as indicated below, using Interface and Operations attributes. Set the value for **Interface** as *com. bb.bloomrentalejb.external.CreditScoreService* and for **Operation** as *getCreditScore*.

Figure 18. The properties pane for the credit service task.

- Generate a PNG file for the process; save the changes and check in.

This completes the process design for the first increment, which has a process with a simple service task to call a method in a Java class, and there are variables defined at the process level and at the task level to carry the data.

3.2. Updating the Application

- Create a domain class called *com.bb.bloomrentaldomain.RentalApp* implementing *java.io.Serializable* in the project *bloom-rental-domain* and define the following member variables with getters and setters.

```
private String firstName;
private String lastName;
private String ssn;
private int creditScore;
```

- Create a POJO *com.bb.bloomrentalejb.external.CreditScoreService* in the *bloom-rental-ejb* project. Implement a method called *getCreditScore()*, as shown below, to create a random number and set it as the credit score for the *RentalApp* instance in the argument.

```
package com.bb.bloomrentalejb.external;
import java.util.Random;
import com.bb.bloomrentaldomain.RentalApp;
public class CreditScoreService {
        private static Random random = new Random();
        public void getCreditScore(Object obj) {
            RentalApp app = (RentalApp) obj;
            Integer num = random.nextInt(300) + 500;
            app.setCreditScore(num);
            System.out.println("CreditScoreService called");
        }
}
```

The jBPM framework discovers this class and method by reflection based on the information provided in the service task design, so it is imperative that

- ○ the class name and the method name exactly match the Interface property and the Operation property of the service task defined in the BPMN process, respectively

- ○ the *getCreditScore()* method has one and only parameter and its of Object type

- Currently in the *startProcess()* method of *ProcessFacade* EJB, the knowledge base is built every time a process is started. This is obviously inefficient, since the process definition is static and does not change in runtime. Ideally a knowledge base should be created during start-up and used by all processes. So create a class called *com. bb.bloomrentalejb.process.KnowledgebaseBuilder* and build the knowledge base there during class loading, as shown below.

```
package com.bb.bloomrentalejb.process;
import org.drools.KnowledgeBase;
import org.drools.builder.KnowledgeBuilder;
import org.drools.builder.KnowledgeBuilderFactory;
import org.drools.builder.ResourceType;
import org.drools.io.ResourceFactory;
public class KnowledgebaseBuilder {
    public static KnowledgeBase kbase;
     static {
       build();
       }
    private static void build() {
       KnowledgeBuilder kbuilder = KnowledgeBuilderFactory.
       newKnowledgeBuilder();
       kbuilder.add(
       ResourceFactory.newClassPathResource("com.bb.bloomrentalapp.
       bpmn2"),
                ResourceType.BPMN2);
       kbase = kbuilder.newKnowledgeBase();
       }
}
```

- The BPMN process is now defined to take input data, which should be passed when the process is started. Modify the *startProcess*() method signature in *ProcessFacadeLocal* EJB to take an additional parameter, *processData*, as shown below.

```
public void startProcess(String processId, Map<String, Object> pro-
cessData);
```

- Modify the *ProcessFacade* EJB to reflect the above change in the *startProcess()* method signature and pass this parameter to *ksession.startProcess()*, as shown below. Since *processData* is a map, it will enable us to pass any variable to the process with a name-value pair.

```java
package com.bb.bloomrentalejb.process;
import java.util.Map;
import javax.ejb.Stateless;
import javax.ejb.TransactionManagement;
import javax.ejb.TransactionManagementType;
import javax.naming.Context;
import javax.naming.InitialContext;
import javax.persistence.EntityManagerFactory;
import javax.persistence.PersistenceUnit;
import javax.transaction.UserTransaction;
import org.drools.KnowledgeBaseFactory;
import org.drools.persistence.jpa.JPAKnowledgeService;
import org.drools.runtime.Environment;
import org.drools.runtime.EnvironmentName;
import org.drools.runtime.StatefulKnowledgeSession;
import org.jbpm.bpmn2.handler.ServiceTaskHandler;
import org.slf4j.Logger;
import org.slf4j.LoggerFactory;
@Stateless
@TransactionManagement(TransactionManagementType.BEAN)
public class ProcessFacade implements ProcessFacadeLocal {
    private static Logger log = LoggerFactory.getLogger(ProcessFacade.
    class);
    @PersistenceUnit(unitName = "jpa.jbpm")
    private EntityManagerFactory emf;
    @Override
    public void startProcess(String processId, Map<String, Object>
    processData) {
       log.info("startProcess called for" + processId);
       startBPM(processId, processData);
    }
```

```java
public void startBPM(String processId, Map<String, Object> processData)
{
        UserTransaction ut = null;
        StatefulKnowledgeSession ksession = null;
        try {
          Context ctx = new InitialContext();
     ut = (UserTransaction) ctx.lookup("java:comp/UserTransaction");
     ut.begin();
     ksession = JPAKnowledgeService.newStatefulKnowledgeSession(
          KnowledgebaseBuilder.kbase, null, createEnvironment());
          ksession.getWorkItemManager().registerWorkItemHandler(
                     "Service Task", new ServiceTaskHandler());
          ksession.startProcess(processId, processData);
          ut.commit();
        } catch (Exception e) {
          e.printStackTrace();
        try {
          ut.rollback();
          } catch (Exception ex) {
          ex.printStackTrace();
          }
        } finally {
          try {
          ksession.dispose();
          } catch (Exception e) {
          e.printStackTrace();
          }
        }
}
private Environment createEnvironment() {
   Environment environment = KnowledgeBaseFactory.newEnvironment();
   environment.set(EnvironmentName.ENTITY_MANAGER_FACTORY, emf);
   return environment;
}
}
```

- The modified *ProcessFacade* EJB code above logs trace statements to the JBOSS log file using *slf4j* library. It gets an instance of *org.slf4j.Logger*, as shown below. Other classes use the same mechanism to get Logger instances and log trace statements.

```
private static Logger log = LoggerFactory.getLogger(ProcessFacade.
class);
```

- As established above, the *startProcess()* method now uses a knowledge base built from *KnowledgeBaseBuilder* as opposed to creating one each time.

- Any task node used in a BPMN process should be bound with a handler class, which will execute when the process hits that node. Such a handler should implement *org.drools.runtime.process.WorkItemHandler* interface which has two methods: *executeWorkItem()* and *abortWorkItem()*. In a normal scenario, *executeWorkItem()* gets called upon when the task node is getting executed. For a service task, the jBPM developers have made it easy for us by providing a ready-made handler called *org.jbpm.bpmn2. handler.ServiceTaskHandler*. While we are not bound to using this, for all basic needs it should suffice. The above implementation of the *startProcess()* method uses this handler, and registers it with the statement below before starting the process. This statement is good enough for any other Service Tasks used in the same process.

```
ksession.getWorkItemManager().registerWorkItemHandler("Service Task",
new ServiceTaskHandler());
```

- The input data required for the process has to come from the front end. So modify *com.bb.bloomrentalejb.processcor.AppProcessor* in the web project to pull information from the HTTP request, build an instance of *RentalApp*, and pass it to EJB as shown below. The first parameter of the *startProcess*() is the ID of the BPMN process to be executed, which in our case is *com.bb.bloomrentalapp.*

```java
package com.bb.bloomrentalweb.processor;
import java.util.HashMap;
import java.util.Map;
import javax.naming.Context;
import javax.naming.InitialContext;
import javax.servlet.http.HttpServletRequest;
import org.slf4j.Logger;
import org.slf4j.LoggerFactory;
import com.bb.bloomrentaldomain.RentalApp;
import com.bb.bloomrentalejb.process.ProcessFacadeLocal;
public class AppProcessor {
private static Logger log = LoggerFactory.getLogger(AppProcessor.
class);
public void processApp(HttpServletRequest request) {
try {
    Context context = new InitialContext();
    ProcessFacadeLocal processFacade = (ProcessFacadeLocal)
    context.lookup("java:module/ProcessFacade");
    RentalApp app = buildProcessData(request);
    Map<String, Object> processData = new HashMap<String, Object>();
    processData.put("app", app);
    processFacade.startProcess("com.bb.bloomrentalapp", processData);
    log.info("Credit Score:" + app.getCreditScore());
} catch (Exception e) {
    e.printStackTrace();
}
}
```

```
private RentalApp buildProcessData(HttpServletRequest request) {
    String firstName = request.getParameter("firstName");
    String lastName = request.getParameter("lastName");
    String ssn = request.getParameter("ssn");
    RentalApp app = new RentalApp();
    app.setFirstName(firstName);
    app.setLastName(lastName);
    app.setSsn(ssn);
    return app;
  }
}
```

- The next stop is the *com.bb.bloomrentalweb.AppServlet* class. Modify the *processApp()* there to pass the incoming *HttpServletRequest* object to the *processor.processApp()* method.

```
public void processApp(HttpServletRequest request, HttpServletResponse
response) throws ServletException, IOException{
    AppProcessor processor = new AppProcessor();
    processor.processApp(request);
    response.sendRedirect("showapp");
}
```

- Modify the *app.jsp* created in chapter 2 to have three fields—first name, last name, and Social Security number, as shown below.

```
<%@page contentType="text/html" pageEncoding="UTF-8"%>
<!DOCTYPE HTML PUBLIC "-//W3C//DTD HTML 4.01 Transitional//EN"
    "http://www.w3.org/TR/html4/loose.dtd">
<html>
<head>
<meta http-equiv="Content-Type" content="text/html; charset=UTF-8">
<link rel="stylesheet" type="text/css" href="${pageContext.request.con-
textPath}/css/style.css"/>
<title>Bloom Apartments</title>
</head>
<body>
    <h2>Rental Application - Hello World</h2>
    <form action="submitapp" method="POST">
     <table border="none">
       <tr>
        <td>First Name</td>
        <td><input type="text" name="firstName" /></td>
       </tr>
       <tr>
        <td>Last Name</td>
        <td><input type="text" name="lastName" /></td>
       </tr>
       <tr>
        <td>SSN</td>
       <td><input type="text" name="ssn" /></td>
      </tr>
      <tr>
       <td colspan="2"><input type="SUBMIT" value="Submit App" /></td>
      </tr>
     </table>
   </form>
</body>
</html>
```

- The above *app.jsp* uses a css with minimal styling. Create a file called *style.css* under *webapp/css* in the *bloom-rental-web* project and copy these contents:

```
table, tr, td{border:none}
.hr50 {
width: 50%;
}
hr {
border-color: black;
margin-left: 0px;
}
body {
font-family: arial;
}
.readonlyinput {
border:none;
width: 30px;
}
```

3.3. Running the Application

Now we are capturing the first name, last name, and Social Security number of each applicant from the front end, putting this information in a domain object and passing it to the jBPM process, which invokes the *CreditScoreService* to determine the credit score (of course, ideally from an external service, but in our case it simply generates a random credit score) and prints it in the log file. Truly speaking, the value entered on the front end is never used in the code. At this time, the only mission of our jBPM process is to invoke this *CreditScoreService* via a service task.

- Download the BPMN2 file (*com.bb.bloomrentalapp.bpmn2*) from the *Web Designer* and put it under *src/main/resources* in *bloom-rental-ejb*.

- Do an `mvn clean install` and deploy.

- Go to the URL http://localhost:8080/bloom-rental/showapp. There's no need to enter any data; just submit the JSP and we should see the console and log file printing a credit score.

Summary

A service task is one of the important features of BPMN, which we just designed, configured, and used in the context of a business use case. It would help your understanding a big deal if you take a look at the source code of the default handler for a service task; *org.jbpm.bpmn2.handler.ServiceTaskHandler* is available at https://github.com/droolsjbpm/jbpm/blob/5.4.0.Final/jbpm-bpmn2/src/main/java/org/jbpm/bpmn2/handler/ServiceTaskHandler.java, and it is pretty straightforward. Feel free to play around with this class by cloning it to create your own handler, tweaking it, and registering the same with the process engine.

CHAPTER 4

THE BLOOM RENTAL APPLICATION: ADDING A RULE TASK

Our Bloom rental application is now at a stage at which we are ready to accept some data from the user interface and are able to kick off a BPMN process, which determines the credit score based on the Social Security number of the applicant (which of course is a made-up number in our case). We want to take it to the next step by adding an ability to the process through which it can make a determination as to whether or not the application is approved based on the credit score. Let's set that magic number as 600. So, we want to dictate that anybody with a credit score of 600 or above is approved; those below that, "better luck next time." A great choice for implementing such a conditional logic is *Drools Rules*. This logic is captured by means of one or more *Drools Rules* and stored as an asset in the knowledge base. Any business process looking to use this set of rules will include what is known as a *Rule Task* and tie it up with one or more business rules defined in the knowledge base.

The development steps here are little long-winded. They include updating the domain class with parameters related to rules, uploading it to *Guvnor* (the *Web Designer*) so it can be used by the assets there, creating the rule, unit testing it, and finally adding a rule node to the process.

4.1. Updating the Domain Class

- Add two Boolean variables, *approvedByRules* and *factUpdated*, to the *RentalApp* domain class with getters and setters. The first variable is to indicate whether or not the candidate is approved, while the purpose of the second variable will be explained later.

```
private boolean approvedByRules = false;
private boolean factUpdated = false;
```

- Remove *App.java* and *AppTest.java* from the *bloom-rental-domain* project created by Maven, since they are not required in this exercise.

- Select **bloom-rental-domain** project in Eclipse, **right click -> Export -> Java -> JAR file** to export the *bloom-rental-domain* project as a JAR file - make sure to include the class files and resources, as shown below.

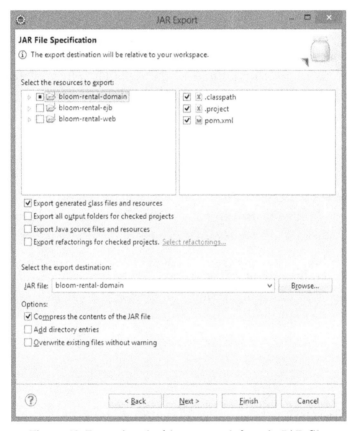

Figure 19. Exporting the bloom-rental-domain JAR file.

4.2. Creating the Model in Guvnor

The domain JAR file just created is the model file and has to be imported into *Guvnor* so that other assets there can make reference to the model classes.

- Since the *RentalApp* domain class is in the package *com.bb.bloomrentaldomain*, we have to first create a package with the same name in *Guvnor* and import the JAR file to that. So, create a new package *com.bb.bloomrentaldomain* in *Guvnor*.

Figure 20. Creating a new package for the model.

- Create a new model *bb-domain* in the package *com.bb.bloomrentaldomain* by selecting **Create New -> Upload POJO Model jar**.

Figure 21. Creating a new model.

- Choose the JAR file created from the above step and upload it. You should see a message: File was uploaded successfully.

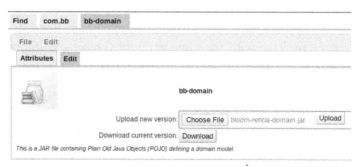

Figure 22. Uploading the JAR file for the domain.

- Save the changes and check in.

4.3. Creating the Rules

- In the *Designer*, click on **Create New -> New Rule**. In the pop-up window, select **DRL Rule (Technical rule–text editor)** and name the rule as *app-selection* to land it in a text editor.

Figure 23. Creating a new DRL rule.

- Copy and paste the code below in the text editor area.

```
import com.bb.bloomrentaldomain.RentalApp;

rule "Credit Score fact update"
ruleflow-group "app-criteria"
dialect "mvel"
salience 100
when
$a:RentalApp(factUpdated == false)
then
System.out.println("Test rule firing...");
$a.setFactUpdated(true);
    update($a);
end

rule "Credit Score above 600"
ruleflow-group "app-criteria"
dialect "mvel"
salience 50
when
$a:RentalApp(creditScore > 600)
then
$a.setApprovedByRules(true);
System.out.println("Credit Score above 600 rule firing..." +
$a.getCreditScore());
end

rule "Credit Score under 600"
ruleflow-group "app-criteria"
dialect "mvel"
salience 40
  when
    $a:RentalApp(creditScore < 600)
then
    $a.setApprovedByRules(false);
    System.out.println("Credit Score under 600 rule
  firing...:" + $a.getCreditScore());
end
```

- A few points to note here:

  - All the rules use only one fact or a piece of information, which is an instance of the *RentalApp*.

  - The **rule flow group**: This is the one and only attribute that binds jBPM and *Drools*. When you define a rule node in the process, you should define its rule flow group; jBPM runtime will look through the knowledge base for the rules that have this matching rule flow attribute and will request that the rule engine execute them.

  - **Salience** prioritizes the rules during execution—the highest number gets first priority.

  - The first rule, *Credit Score Fact update*, serves the purpose of updating the fact in the rule engine, giving an opportunity for the rules to activate again based on the latest information available.

  - When used in the context of a jBPM process, the rules get activated (meaning the *when* conditions are evaluated) as soon as the associated facts are inserted into the session (which is typically before the start of process); they will be executed (meaning that the *then* part is processed) only when the process execution hits the rule task node. This is fine as long as the facts remain static until the rule task node is encountered. But if the value of facts changes between the time that the *when* condition is evaluated and the *then* part is processed, we want to make sure that the rules are activated (meaning that the *when* condition is evaluated) again with the latest available information. The first rule accomplishes exactly that by calling on *update()*. Further, in order to avoid a cyclical execution, we use the *factUpdated* property, which will ensure that the first rule gets executed only once.

- On the left-hand side, clicking on **Fact types** should show the *RentalApp* class and its members, which are made available through the uploaded JAR file:

```
Fact types:(hide)        import com.bb.bloomrentaldomain.RentalApp;
⊟ ⓘ RentalApp
                         rule "Credit Score fact update"
   ⬥ this               ruleflow-group "app-criteria"
                         dialect "mvel"
   ⬥ approvedByRules     salience 100
                         when
   ⬥ creditScore               $a:RentalApp(factUpdated == false)
   ⬥ factUpdated         then
                               System.out.println("Fact update rule firing...");
   ⬥ firstName                 $a.setFactUpdated(true);
                               update($a);
   ⬥ lastName            end

   ⬥ ssn                rule "Credit Score above 600"
                         ruleflow-group "app-criteria"
                         dialect "mvel"
                         salience 50
                         when
                               $a:RentalApp( creditScore > 600 )
                         then
                               $a.setRuleSelected(true);
                               System.out.println("Credit Score above 600 rule firing..." + $a.getCreditScore());
                         end

                         rule "Credit Score under 600"
```

Figure 24. The rule editor in the designer.

- Save the changes and check in.

4.4. Unit Testing the Rules

It will save us a lot of trouble if we unit test the rules in *Guvnor* itself.

- **Create New -> New Test Scenarios.**

Figure 25. Creating a new test scenario.

- Name it *app-selection-test*; leave the package as *com.bb.bloomrentaldomain* and click **OK** to enter the Edit tab of the test scenario as shown below.

Figure 26. The Edit tab of the test scenario.

This screen takes a mock-up input data set and gives the expected output. It runs the test scenario and declares that the test passed or failed depending on whether or not the actual output matched the expected output.

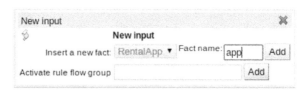

Figure 27. Input for the test scenario.

- Click on the plus sign (+) beside GIVEN. Enter the Fact name as *app* and click **Add**.

- Click on the same plus sign (+) beside GIVEN. Enter the **Activate rule flow group** as *'app-criteria'* and click **Add**.

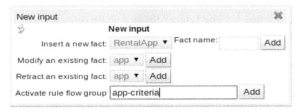

Figure 28. The rule flow group for the test scenario.

- Click on the **Add a Field** link under **Insert 'RentalApp'[app]**. Choose the *factUp-dated* field and click OK.

Figure 29. Adding a field for the test scenario.

- Click on the pencil icon next to the *factUpdated* field and click on **Literal Value** in the pop-up box.

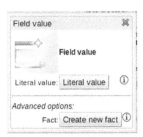

Figure 30. The Field Value for the test scenario.

- Select *false* from the drop-down menu for **factUpdated**.

Figure 31. The Literal Value for the test scenario.

- Click on **Insert 'RentalApp'[app]** again. Choose *creditScore* and click **OK**.

Figure 32. Choosing a field for the test scenario.

- Click on the pencil icon next to the **creditScore** field and click on *Literal Value* in the pop-up box.

- Enter a value of 700 for **creditScore**.

Figure 33. Entering a value for the test scenario.

- We have created a mock-up instance in *RentalApp*, named it *app*, and set its member variables *factUpdated* and *creditScore* to false and 700, respectively. We also have noted that our intention is to activate the *app-criteria* rule flow group. The next step is to set the expected result set when the *app-criteria* rule group is executed with a mock *RentalApp* instance. Click on the plus sign (+) beside EXPECT now and click on **Add** against **Fact value**.

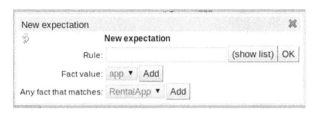

Figure 34. The expectation for the test scenario.

- Click on the green icon next to **RentalApp 'app' has values.**

Figure 35. The green icon for a fact value.

- Select *approvedbyRules* and click **OK**.

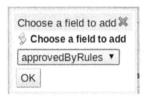

Figure 36. Choosing a field to add for the test scenario.

- Leave a value of *true* for **approvedbyRules**. The test scenario should look like this:

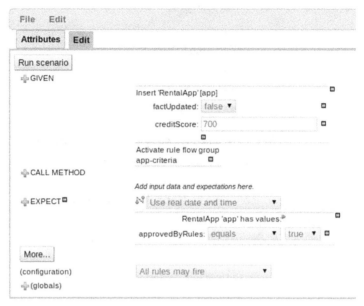

Figure 37. The test scenario.

- Click on Run scenario. It should show results in green with 100 percent completion and a summary of output as shown below. The obvious interpretation is that the rule engine approves a candidate with a credit score of 700 or higher.

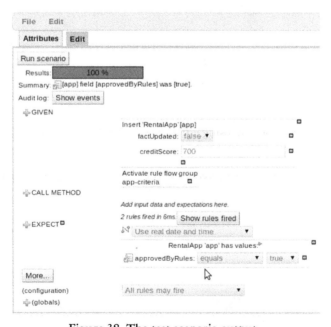

Figure 38. The test scenario output.

- Now change the input **creditScore** to 400 and the expected **approvedByRules** to false. Click **Run scenario** to get a pass again. The interpretation here is that a candidate with a credit score of 400 will be rejected by the rule engine.

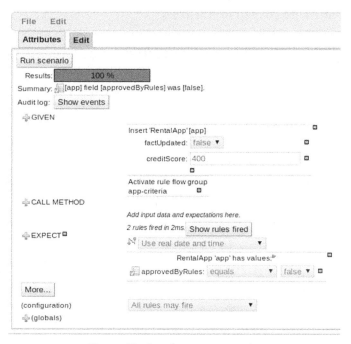

Figure 39. Another test scenario.

- Save the changes and check in.

4.5. Designing the Process

A unit-tested rule is a good enough candidate for the BPM process to use.

- Open the *bloomrentalapp* business process.

- Delete the end event, select the *Credit Service Task*, and connect another task to it.

- Select the new task added and click on the tool icon to see the list of available tasks; select *Business Rule Task* there.

- Select the rule task; name the task *App Selection Task* and set the **ruleflow-group** property to *app-criteria*. Remember the value of *ruleflow-group* should match the *ruleflow-group* attribute defined for the rules.

- Follow the rule task with an end event. The process should look like that shown below.

- Save the changes and check in.

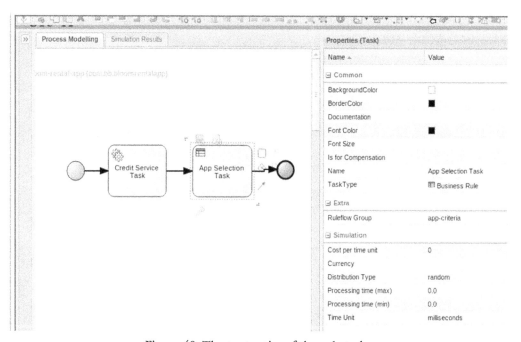

Figure 40. The properties of the rule task.

4.6. Using the Process

- Copy the BPMN2 file in the XML version from *Guvnor* and overlay it on the contents of *com.bb.bloomrentalapp.bpmn2* at *src/main/resources* under *bloom-rental-ejb*.

- Create a new file called *app-selection.drl* beside *com.bb.bloomrentalapp.bpmn2*.

- Copy the contents of *app-selection.drl* from *Guvnor* and put them in the file created in the *bloom-rental-ejb* project.

- Go to the *KnowledgeBaseBuilder* class and update the *build()* method to add *app-selection.drl* method to the knowledge base, as shown below.

```
package com.bb.bloomrentalejb.process;
import org.drools.KnowledgeBase;
import org.drools.builder.KnowledgeBuilder;
import org.drools.builder.KnowledgeBuilderFactory;
import org.drools.builder.ResourceType;
import org.drools.io.ResourceFactory;
public class KnowledgebaseBuilder {
    public static KnowledgeBase kbase;
        static {
        build();
        }
    private static void build() {
        KnowledgeBuilder kbuilder = KnowledgeBuilderFactory
                        .newKnowledgeBuilder();
        kbuilder.add(ResourceFactory
        .newClassPathResource("com.bb.bloomrentalapp.bpmn2"),
                        ResourceType.BPMN2);
        kbuilder.add(ResourceFactory.newClassPathResource("app-selec-
        tion.drl"), ResourceType.DRL);
        kbase = kbuilder.newKnowledgeBase();
    }
}
```

- The data used in the evaluation part (the *when* part) of the Drools rules is referred as *fact*, which has to be inserted into the rule engine separately. Again the facts have to come from the application. Let's get the EJB ready for that. Change the signature of the *startProcess()* method in *ProcessFacadeLocal* to take an additional parameter for facts of type *List<Object>*, as shown below.

```
public void startProcess(String processId, Map<String, Object> pro-
cessData, List<Object> facts);
```

- Change the signature and implementation of the *startProcess()* and *startBPM ()* methods in the *ProcessFacade* EJB accordingly and insert the available facts into *ksession* before starting the process and call *ksession.fireAllRules()* after starting the process to activate all matching rules.

```
public void startProcess(String processId, Map<String, Object> pro-
cessData, List<Object> facts) {
        log.info("startProcess called for" + processName);
        startBPM(processId, processData, facts);
}
public void startBPM(String processId, Map<String, Object> processData,
List<Object> facts) {
....
    for(Object fact:facts) {
        ksession.insert(fact);
    }
    ksession.startProcess(processId, processData);
    ksession.fireAllRules();

}
```

- Modify the *processApp()* method in *AppProcessor* to build fact, which is nothing but a *RentalApp* instance, and pass it on to the *startProcess()* method as an argument.

```
public void processApp(HttpServletRequest request)
{
    ....
    RentalApp app = buildProcessData(request);
    Map<String, Object> processData = new HashMap<String, Object>();
    processData.put("app", app);
    List<Object> facts = new ArrayList<Object>();
    facts.add(app);
    processFacade.startProcess("com.bb.bloomrentalapp", processData,
    facts);
    ....
}
```

- That's it! No change is needed in the *AppServlet*. Do an mvn clean install and deploy.

- Access the application and submit the form; the process should now execute properly. Depending on the value of the credit score, *RentalApp.approvedByRules* should be true or false. The log file should show which rule is being executed.

Summary

A service task and a rule task from Hello World—not bad, right? Though we used a rule task and coded a few simple rules, we did not dive deep into *Drools*, which is a separate subject by itself. It could get pretty rough if you try to use *Drools* without quite understanding how jBPM and *Drools* work together. The directions in this chapter should have set you on the right path.

CHAPTER 5

THE BLOOM RENTAL APPLICATION: ADDING A HUMAN TASK AND A SERVICE TASK

The different versions of the Bloom rental application process created so far are short-running ones, meaning that once the process is initiated it goes all the way to the finish line automatically within a few milliseconds. Now we are going to make the process a long-running one by adding a step in the process called the *human task*, which requires a manual intervention to progress forward.

The term *human task* had me a little intrigued when I heard it the first time. How can a human perform a task as a part of business process? It made sense later when I realized that it is a task performed by a person through a user interface that forms a step of the business process. The process would start as usual and come to a halt upon hitting the human task, at which point somebody will have to look at the state of the process and make a determination that will control its further direction. In this chapter we get little ahead of ourselves: in addition to the human task step, we will also develop the next step for a service task. This way, with the completion of the human task, we can see another node getting executed as opposed to the process getting finished, so we can get more insight on the completion state of the human task.

The implementation gets a bit more involved here compared to earlier chapters, so we will break it down into small steps as shown below.

- Designing the process to add a human task node.

- Adding a service task.

- Modifying the application code to be able to use the process.

- Designing the human task form to display the task list and act on it.

- Putting them all together.

5.1. Adding a Human Task Node

This is probably the easiest section in this chapter.

- In the *Designer*, open the process created in chapter 4 and, from the properties pane, add a process variable called *admin* of type *com.bb.bloomrentaldomain.RentalAdmin*, as shown below. This class, which will be created later, is used to capture information related to the human task such as its owner, approval status, and comments.

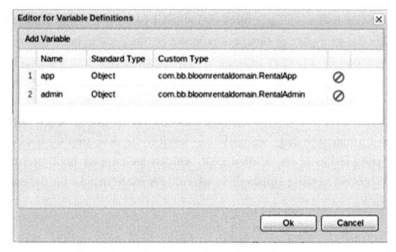

Figure 41. Adding a second variable to the process.

- Delete the end event; select the *App Selection Task* and click on the task icon from the context-sensitive palette. Now select the newly dropped-in task and click on the tool icon to pull the list of available tasks; select *User Task*. By the way, a human task is referred to as a *User Task* in the BPMN terminology. Name the user task *Manual Review Task* and add additional properties to the user task as shown below.

○ Set **Actors** to the MVEL expression #*{admin.reviewUserid}*; this identifies the person who this task is assigned to.

○ The **DataInputSet** is as shown below. Have the task accept a parameter named *inAdmin* of type *com.bb.bloomrentaldomain.RentalAdmin.*

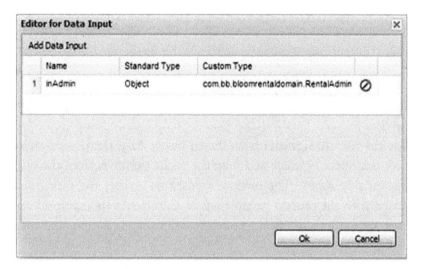

Figure 42. Data input for the reviewer human task.

○ The **DataOutputSet** is as shown below. It defines the task to produce an output variable *outAdmin* of type *com.bb.bloomrentaldomain.RentalAdmin*.w\

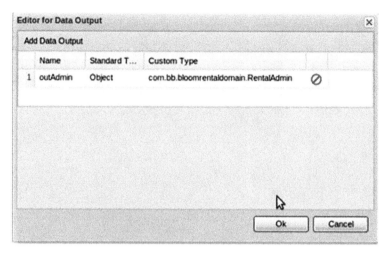

Figure 43. The data output for the reviewer human task.

- Declare the data **Assignments** as shown below. Map the process variable *admin* to the task parameter *inAdmin* and map the result *outAdmin* from the task back to the process variable *admin*. The obvious translation is that the task input *inAdmin* is populated with the process variable *admin*. Comments and approval status from the reviewer are fed into *inAdmin*, copied as *outAdmin*, outputted, and mapped back to the process variable *admin*.

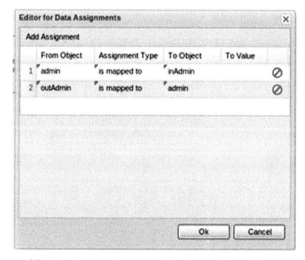

Figure 44. The data assignments for the reviewer human task.

○ Define **Task Name** as *Manual Review Task*, as shown below.

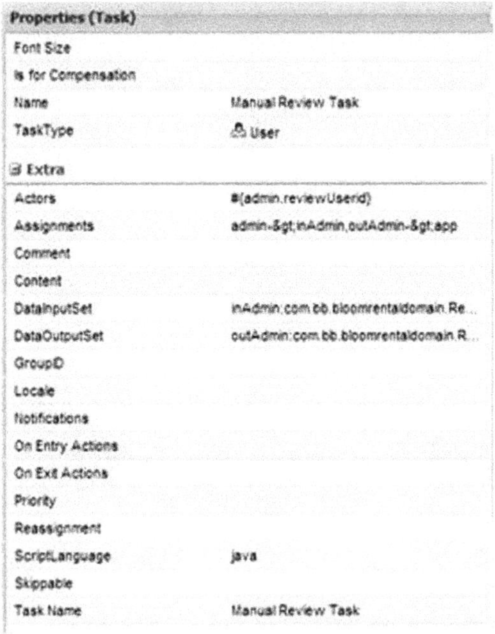

Properties (Task)

Font Size	
Is for Compensation	
Name	Manual Review Task
TaskType	� User
⊟ Extra	
Actors	#{admin.reviewUserId}
Assignments	admin->inAdmin,outAdmin->app
Comment	
Content	
DataInputSet	inAdmin:com.bb.bloomrentaldomain.Re...
DataOutputSet	outAdmin:com.bb.bloomrentaldomain.R...
GroupID	
Locale	
Notifications	
On Entry Actions	
On Exit Actions	
Priority	
Reassignment	
ScriptLanguage	java
Skippable	
Task Name	Manual Review Task

Figure 45. The task name for the reviewer human task.

○ For the user to take action on human task, there should be a user interface where he or she can look at the information related to that task. The *Web Designer* presents a way to design such an interface easily and it is called *task form*. Any user task in the process should be associated with what is called a *task form* to avoid validation error. So let's create it even though we will not be using it in our exercise. Select the *Manual Review Task* and select the **Edit Task Form** icon on the context palette as shown below.

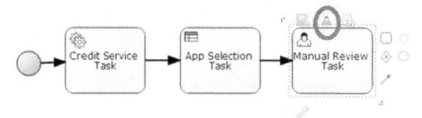

Figure 46. The Edit Task Form icon for the user task.

- This will take us to the Task Form editor, as shown below. Save it with no contents.

Figure 47. The Task Form editor.

- Save the changes and check in.

5.2. Adding a Service Task to Follow the Human Task

Upon successful completion of the human task, we want to send out a letter to the applicant to notify him or her of the decision. This can be achieved by a service task similar to the

Credit Service Task. Again, for the purposes of our exercise we will not really send out a letter; instead we will simply print out a log statement. In the real world, a more sophisticated service can be used to draft a nice letter and dispatch it. Now that we are at the professional level with the service task, we can move on to the higher-level instructions.

- Add a service task node next to the manual review task and set its properties as shown below.

    ○ **Name**: Letter Dispatch Service.

    ○ **DataInputSet**: Parameter–Object.

    ○ **Assignment**: admin is mapped to Parameter.

    ○ **Interface**: *com.bb.bloomrentalejb.external.LetterDispatchService.*

    ○ **Operation**: *sendLetter.*

- Connect the *Letter Dispatch Service* to an end event.

- Save the changes and check in.

With the manual review task and letter dispatch tasks, the process should appear as follows:

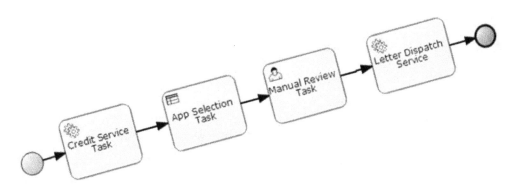

Figure 48. The Bloom rental process with a manual review task.

5.3. Modifying the Application Code

- Create the class *com.bb.bloomrentaldomain.RentalAdmin*, implementing *java.io.Serializable* in the *bloom-rental-domain* project; then define a String variable *reviewUserid*. The process is designed for the actor attribute of the manual review task to be pointing to *#{admin.reviewUserId}*, which actually would resolve to this variable defined in *RentalAdmin* class. When a reviewer looks at the application and the decision of the rule engine, he or she may choose to accept it or override it and add some comments justifying that decision. To capture these data, define a Boolean variable *approvedByReviewer* and a String variable *reviewerComments*. Make sure this class has getters and setters for all variables.

```
private String reviewUserid;
private boolean approvedByreviewer;
private String reviewerComments;
```

- Create the Service class *com.bb.bloomrentalejb.external.LetterDispatchService* with a method *sendLetter(Object)* to print the status of the human task as shown below.

```
package com.bb.bloomrentalejb.external;
import org.slf4j.Logger;
import org.slf4j.LoggerFactory;
import com.bb.bloomrentaldomain.RentalAdmin;

public class LetterDispatchService {
private static Logger log = LoggerFactory.
getLogger(LetterDispatchService.class);

public void sendLetter(Object param) {
        log.info("Calling from LetterDispatchService...");
        RentalAdmin admin = (RentalAdmin)param;
        log.info("The reviewer has" + (admin.isApprovedByreviewer()?"a
        pproved":"rejected")
                + "the task with the following comments:");
        log.info(admin.getReviewerComments());
}
}
```

- The variable *reviewUserid* in *RentalAdmin* class that was just defined has to be populated with a literal value. In other words, the reviewer has to be identified at some point. In a real-world application, we can have different mechanisms that do that depending on the business use case. But here, for our exercise, we want to simply drop it in the *AppProcessor* class. Write a method *buildRentalAdmin()* in *com.bb.bloomrentalweb. controller.AppProcessor* to create an instance of *RentalAdmin* with the reviewer user ID hardcoded to *Reviewer* as shown below. Put the *RentalAdmin* instance into *processData*, which gets injected into the business process.

```
public void processApp(HttpServletRequest request)
{
    ..........
    RentalApp app = buildProcessData(request);
    Map<String, Object> processData = new HashMap<String, Object>();
    processData.put("app", app);
    processData.put("admin", buildRentalAdmin());
    .............
}
private RentalAdmin buildRentalAdmin()
{
    RentalAdmin admin = new RentalAdmin();
    admin.setReviewUserid("Reviewer");
    return admin;
}
```

5.3.1. The Task Server

When the process engine encounters a human task, it will try to assign the task to the designated user. When the assigned user takes action on the task, the task will be completed. These two different activities of assigning/creating a task and completing a task are carried out by what is called a task server. jBPM provides few choices for a task server; we will be using the local task server implementation, which is bundled with the jBPM package. The local task server implementation runs in the same JVM as the calling program and processes each request synchronously. We will provide a layer around that local task server for our convenience.

- In *bloom-rental-ejb* project, define an interface called *com.bb.bloomrentalejb.task.TaskServer* to define *start()* and *stop()* operations as in the box below.

```
package com.bb.bloomrentalejb.task;

public interface TaskServer {
    public void start();
    public void stop();
}
```

- Create *com.bb.bloomrentalejb.task.LocalTaskServer* to implement *TaskServer*, which will be used as a wrapper to call the jBPM task server. This class will host the *EntityManagerFactory* statically; *start()* will instantiate the underlying task engine and *stop()* will close the *EntityManagerFactory* instance. So *start()* should be called before the first use of the task server and *stop()* should be called before the application shuts down. Implement *start()* and *stop()* as shown below.

```
package com.bb.bloomrentalejb.task;
import javax.persistence.EntityManagerFactory;
import javax.persistence.Persistence;
import org.drools.SystemEventListenerFactory;

public class LocalTaskServer implements TaskServer {
    private static EntityManagerFactory emf =
        Persistence.createEntityManagerFactory("jpa.jbpm.task");
    private static org.jbpm.task.service.TaskService _instance;
    public static org.jbpm.task.service.TaskService getService() {
    return startService();
    }
private static org.jbpm.task.service.TaskService startService() {
    if (_instance == null) {
        _instance = new org.jbpm.task.service.TaskService(emf,
        SystemEventListenerFactory.getSystemEventListener());
    }
    return _instance;
}
@Override
public void start() {
    _instance = startService();
}
@Override
public void stop(){
    if (emf != null) {
      emf.close();
      emf = null;
      }
    }
}
```

As you can see, this class keeps a reference of the task engine, *org.jbpm.task.service.TaskService*, which is a singleton object and issues the same instance to all requestors. Note that the

TaskService class is used with full qualified name. This is to avoid ambiguity with another interface, *org.jbpm.task.TaskService*, which is not referenced here and is internally used by the implementation.

- The entity manager factory is using a different persistence unit here, which should be defined in *persistence.xml* as shown below.

```xml
<persistence-unit name="jpa.jbpm.task" transaction-type="JTA">
  <provider>org.hibernate.ejb.HibernatePersistence</provider>
  <jta-data-source>java:jboss/datasources/bloomDS</jta-data-source>
  <mapping-file>META-INF/JBPMorm.xml</mapping-file>
  <mapping-file>META-INF/ProcessInstanceInfo.hbm.xml</mapping-file>
  <mapping-file>META-INF/Taskorm.xml</mapping-file>
  <!-- Session -->
  <class>org.drools.persistence.info.SessionInfo</class>
    <class>org.jbpm.persistence.processinstance.ProcessInstanceInfo</class>
  <class>org.drools.persistence.info.WorkItemInfo</class>
    <!-- Tasks -->
  <class>org.jbpm.task.Attachment</class>
  <class>org.jbpm.task.Content</class>
  <class>org.jbpm.task.BooleanExpression</class>
  <class>org.jbpm.task.Comment</class>
  <class>org.jbpm.task.Deadline</class>
  <class>org.jbpm.task.Comment</class>
  <class>org.jbpm.task.Deadline</class>
  <class>org.jbpm.task.Delegation</class>
  <class>org.jbpm.task.Escalation</class>
  <class>org.jbpm.task.Group</class>
  <class>org.jbpm.task.I18NText</class>
  <class>org.jbpm.task.Notification</class>
  <class>org.jbpm.task.EmailNotification</class>
  <class>org.jbpm.task.EmailNotificationHeader</class>
  <class>org.jbpm.task.PeopleAssignments</class>
```

```xml
    <class>org.jbpm.task.Reassignment</class>
      <class>org.jbpm.task.Status</class>
      <class>org.jbpm.task.Task</class>
      <class>org.jbpm.task.TaskData</class>
      <class>org.jbpm.task.SubTasksStrategy</class>
      <class>org.jbpm.task.OnParentAbortAllSubTasksEndStrategy</class>
      <class>org.jbpm.task.OnAllSubTasksEndParentEndStrategy</class>
      <class>org.jbpm.task.User</class>
    <properties>
      <property name="hibernate.dialect" value="org.hibernate.dialect.
      MySQLDialect"/>
      <property name="hibernate.max_fetch_depth" value="3"/>
      <property name="hibernate.hbm2ddl.auto" value="update"/>
      <property name="hibernate.show_sql" value="true"/>
      <property name="hibernate.transaction.manager_lookup_class"

value="org.hibernate.transaction.JBossTransactionManagerLookup"/>
        <property name="hibernate.connection.driver_class" value="com.
        mysql.jdbc.Driver"/>
    </properties>
  </persistence-unit>
```

- As mentioned earlier, all tasks in a process need a work item handler, and a human task is no exception. Fortunately, jBPM provides a handler for a human task; we will create a helper class called *com.bb.bloomrentalejb.task.HumanTaskHelper* to create and supply this handler provided by jBPM as shown below.

```
package com.bb.bloomrentalejb.task;
import org.drools.runtime.KnowledgeRuntime;
import org.drools.runtime.process.WorkItemHandler;
import org.jbpm.process.workitem.wsht.LocalHTWorkItemHandler;
import org.jbpm.task.service.local.LocalTaskService;
public class HumanTaskHelper {
        private static org.jbpm.task.service.TaskService service;
        private static LocalTaskService localTaskService;
        static {
                try {
                        service = LocalTaskServer.getService();
                        localTaskService = new LocalTaskService(service);
                } catch (Exception e) {
                        e.printStackTrace();
                }
        }
        public static WorkItemHandler getLocalWorkItemHandler(Knowled
        geRuntime session) throws Exception {
                return new LocalHTWorkItemHandler(localTaskService,
                session);
        }
        public static LocalTaskService getLocalTaskService() throws
        Exception {
                return localTaskService;
        }
}
```

The local human task handler (*LocalHTWorkItemHandler*) referenced here requires *LocalTaskService* and a knowledge session for construction, where session points to the session of the process in flight and *LocalTaskService* is the static singleton object defined in the *HumanTaskHelper* class. *LocalTaskService* requires, in turn, a *TaskService* class that is provided by the *LocalTaskServer*.

- Before starting the process in *ProcessFacade* EJB, register the human task work item handler while registering the handler for the service task, as shown below.

```
ksession.getWorkItemManager().registerWorkItemHandler("Service Task",
new ServiceTaskHandler());

ksession.getWorkItemManager().registerWorkItemHandler("Human Task",
HumanTaskHelper.getLocalWorkItemHandler(ksession));
```

- Currently the knowledge session is disposed of in *ProcessFacade* after calling up the *ksession.startProcess()*, which is because up to now the process was a short-running one. Now, with the human task, the process is in a waiting state; it is going to be a long-running one, and the *ksession* can be disposed of here only conditionally. And an attempt should be made to dispose of it after resuming from the waiting state, which will be explained in the next section. For now, change the final block in the *startProcess()* method in *ProcessFacade* as shown below. The knowledge session is disposed of only if the process instance is completed. Note that the *ProcessInstance* referred to here is from the package *org.drools.runtime.process*.

```java
public void startBPM(String processName, Map<String, Object> pro-
cessData, List<Object> facts) {
UserTransaction ut = null;
ProcessInstance processInstance = null;
StatefulKnowledgeSession ksession = null;
try {
    Context ctx = new InitialContext();
    ut = (UserTransaction) ctx.lookup("java:comp/UserTransaction");
    ut.begin();
    ksession = JPAKnowledgeService.newStatefulKnowledgeSession(
                    KnowledgebaseBuilder.kbase, null,
                                createEnvironment());
    ksession.getWorkItemManager().registerWorkItemHandler(
                    "Service Task", new ServiceTaskHandler());
    ksession.getWorkItemManager().registerWorkItemHandler("Human Task",
    HumanTaskHelper.getLocalWorkItemHandler(ksession));
    for (Object fact : facts) {
            ksession.insert(fact);
    }
    processInstance = ksession.startProcess(processName, processData);
    ksession.fireAllRules();
    ut.commit();
} catch (Exception e) {
    e.printStackTrace();
    try {
     ut.rollback();
    } catch (Exception ex) {
     ex.printStackTrace();
    }
} finally {
  try {
    if (processInstance != null
      && (processInstance.getState() ==
          ProcessInstance.STATE_COMPLETED)) {
      ksession.dispose();
      }
    }catch (Exception e) {
      e.printStackTrace();
      }
}
}
```

- As noted earlier, the *start()* and *stop()* methods of *TaskServer* should be called upon at the right place; *ServletContextListener* is a good choice. Create a class *com.bb.bloomrentalweb. listener.WebContextListener* to implement *ServletContextListener* as shown below. The *contextInitialized()* method starts the *TaskServer* and *contextDestroyed()* stops the *TaskServer*.

```java
package com.bb.bloomrentalweb.listener;
import javax.servlet.ServletContextEvent;
import javax.servlet.ServletContextListener;
import javax.servlet.annotation.WebListener;
import com.bb.bloomrentalejb.task.LocalTaskServer;
import com.bb.bloomrentalejb.task.TaskServer;
@WebListener
public class WebContextListener implements ServletContextListener{
    @Override
    public void contextDestroyed(ServletContextEvent event) {
     TaskServer taskServer = new LocalTaskServer();
     try {
       taskServer.stop();
     } catch (Exception e) {
       e.printStackTrace();
       throw new RuntimeException("Human Task Server could not be
       started" +
                  "- Application will not function properly");
     }
    }
@Override
public void contextInitialized(ServletContextEvent event) {
    TaskServer taskServer = new LocalTaskServer();
    try {
        taskServer.start();
    } catch (Exception e) {
        e.printStackTrace();
        throw new RuntimeException("Human Task Server could not
        be started" +
        "- Application will not function properly");
        }
    }
}
```

5.3.2. Displaying the Task

The previous section set up the necessary infrastructure to create a task and start the task server. So with this, once the process is initiated and a human task node is encountered, it will automatically assign the task to the designated user. The next step is to display the task to the assigned user so he or she can act on it. This is a simple step. All we need to do is query the task table based on the user ID to get a list of tasks assigned and display the results. There is also an API from jBPM to pull up the tasks.

- Create *com.bb.bloomrentaldomain.RentalTaskData* in the *bloom-rental-domain* project implementing *java.io.Serializable* and define the following member variables with getters and setters. This domain object will be used to capture all details related to a task.

```
private long taskId;
private String taskName;
private RentalApp app;
```

- Now we will need to create and load knowledge sessions from different parts of the application. It will be very helpful to have a helper class that can do that, so we can re-use this code where needed. Create a Stateless Session EJB called *com.bb.bloomrentalejb.session.SessionFacade* with a local interface *com.bb.bloomrentalejb.session.SessionFacadeLocal*.

- Define the methods below in *SessionFacadeLocal*. The *createSession*() method creates a brand new session from a given knowledge base and the *loadSession*() method loads an existing session of given ID using the knowledge base.

```
package com.bb.bloomrentalejb.session;
import javax.ejb.Local;
import org.drools.KnowledgeBase;
import org.drools.runtime.StatefulKnowledgeSession;

@Local
public interface SessionFacadeLocal {
    public StatefulKnowledgeSession createSession(KnowledgeBase
    kbase);
    public StatefulKnowledgeSession loadSession(KnowledgeBase kbase,
            int sessionId);
}
```

- Implement *SessionFacade* as shown below, indicating that it uses Bean Managed Transaction.

```
package com.bb.bloomrentalejb.session;
import javax.ejb.Stateless;
import javax.ejb.TransactionManagement;
import javax.ejb.TransactionManagementType;
import javax.persistence.EntityManagerFactory;
import javax.persistence.PersistenceUnit;
import org.drools.KnowledgeBase;
import org.drools.KnowledgeBaseFactory;
import org.drools.persistence.jpa.JPAKnowledgeService;
import org.drools.runtime.Environment;
import org.drools.runtime.EnvironmentName;
import org.drools.runtime.StatefulKnowledgeSession;
import org.slf4j.Logger;
import org.slf4j.LoggerFactory;
import com.bb.bloomrentalejb.process.KnowledgebaseBuilder;
```

```
@Stateless
@TransactionManagement(TransactionManagementType.BEAN)
public class SessionFacade implements SessionFacadeLocal {
    private static Logger log = LoggerFactory.
    getLogger(SessionFacade.class);
    @PersistenceUnit(unitName = "jpa.jbpm")
    private EntityManagerFactory emf;

    @Override
    public StatefulKnowledgeSession createSession(KnowledgeBase kbase)
    {
        log.info("Creating jbpm session..");
        return JPAKnowledgeService.newStatefulKnowledgeSession(
                KnowledgebaseBuilder.kbase, null,
                createEnvironment());
    }

    @Override
    public StatefulKnowledgeSession loadSession(KnowledgeBase
    kbase, int sessionId) {
        log.info("Loading jbpm session with id" + sessionId);
        return JPAKnowledgeService.loadStatefulKnowledgeSession(
                sessionId, kbase, null, createEnvironment());
    }

    private Environment createEnvironment() {
    Environment environment =
    KnowledgeBaseFactory.newEnvironment();
    environment.set(EnvironmentName.ENTITY_MANAGER_FACTORY,
    emf);
    return environment;
    }
}
```

- Since there is a helper class to create a knowledge session, let's use it in *ProcessFacade* EJB as shown below. Inject the *SessionFacade* EJB and call up its *createSession()* method from the *startBPM*() method. Also remove the *createEnvironment*() method from the *ProcessFacade* EJB.

```
@Stateless
@TransactionManagement(TransactionManagementType.BEAN)
public class ProcessFacade implements ProcessFacadeLocal {
    ....
    @EJB(lookup = "java:module/SessionFacade")
    private SessionFacadeLocal sessionFacade;
    ....
    public void startBPM(String processId, Map<String, Object>
    processData,
                         List<Object> facts) {
    UserTransaction ut = null;
    ProcessInstance processInstance = null;
    StatefulKnowledgeSession ksession = null;
    try {
      Context ctx = new InitialContext();
      ut = (UserTransaction) ctx.lookup("java:comp/UserTransaction");
      ut.begin();
      ksession = sessionFacade.createSession(KnowledgebaseBuilder.
      kbase);
      ksession.getWorkItemManager().registerWorkItemHandler(
                         "Service Task", new ServiceTaskHandler());
      ......
}
```

- Create a Stateless Session EJB called *com.bb.bloomrentalejb.task.TaskFacade* with a local interface *com.bb.bloomrentalejb.task.TaskFacadeLocal* to deal with task-related functionalities. Define the method *getAssignedTasks()* in the *TaskFacadeLocal* interface with the signature given below. This will return all tasks assigned to a given user ID.

```
package com.bb.bloomrentalejb.task;
import java.util.List;
import javax.ejb.Local;
import com.bb.bloomrentaldomain.RentalTaskData;

@Local
public interface TaskFacadeLocal {
public List<RentalTaskData> getAssignedTasks(String userId);
}
```

- Indicate that *com.bb.bloomrentalejb.task.TaskFacade* uses Bean Managed Transaction, and inject *SessionFacade* EJB into a member variable as shown below.

```
package com.bb.bloomrentalejb.task;
import java.util.ArrayList;
import java.util.List;
import javax.ejb.EJB;
import javax.ejb.Stateless;
import javax.ejb.TransactionManagement;
import javax.ejb.TransactionManagementType;
import org.drools.runtime.StatefulKnowledgeSession;
import org.drools.runtime.process.ProcessInstance;
import org.drools.runtime.process.WorkflowProcessInstance;
import org.jbpm.task.Status;
import org.jbpm.task.Task;
import org.jbpm.task.query.TaskSummary;
import org.jbpm.task.service.local.LocalTaskService;
import org.slf4j.Logger;
import org.slf4j.LoggerFactory;
import com.bb.bloomrentaldomain.RentalApp;
import com.bb.bloomrentaldomain.RentalTaskData;
import com.bb.bloomrentalejb.process.KnowledgebaseBuilder;
import com.bb.bloomrentalejb.session.SessionFacadeLocal;

@Stateless
@TransactionManagement(TransactionManagementType.BEAN)
public class TaskFacade implements TaskFacadeLocal {
        private static Logger log = LoggerFactory.
        getLogger(TaskFacade.class);
        @EJB(lookup="java:module/SessionFacade")
        private SessionFacadeLocal sessionFacade;
        @Override
        public List<RentalTaskData> getAssignedTasks(String userId) {
            List<RentalTaskData> data = new
            ArrayList<RentalTaskData>();
            try {
            LocalTaskService service = HumanTaskHelper.
            getLocalTaskService();
            List<Status> status = new ArrayList<Status>();
            //retrieve only Reserved Tasks
```

```
            status.add(Status.Reserved);
            List<TaskSummary> res = service.getTasksOwned(userId,
            status, "en-UK");
            for (Object each : res) {
            TaskSummary t = (TaskSummary) each;
            Task task = service.getTask(t.getId());
            RentalApp app = (RentalApp) getProcessData(task);
            data.add(buildRentalTaskData(t, app));
        }
        } catch (Exception e) {
            e.printStackTrace();
        }
        return data;
    }

    private Object getProcessData(Task task) {
    StatefulKnowledgeSession ksession =
                        sessionFacade.loadSession(KnowledgebaseBu
                        ilder.kbase,
                            task.getTaskData().
                            getProcessSessionId());
    ProcessInstance pi = ((org.drools.runtime.process.
    ProcessRuntime)ksession).
                getProcessInstance(task.getTaskData().
                getProcessInstanceId());
    WorkflowProcessInstance wf = (WorkflowProcessInstance)pi;
    Object obj = wf.getVariable("app");
    return obj;
    }

    private RentalTaskData buildRentalTaskData(TaskSummary task,
    RentalApp app) {
    RentalTaskData data = new RentalTaskData();
    data.setApp(app);
    data.setTaskId(task.getId());
    data.setTaskName(task.getName());
    log.info("RentalTaskData:" + data);
    return data;
        }
}
```

- A task-related data encompasses process variables too. At the time of reviewing the case, the reviewer would need the applicant's detailed information. The *getProcess-Data*() method in *TaskFacade* pulls the *RentalApp* instance associated with the task/process.

- Implement *getAssignedTasks* () in *TaskFacade* to retrieve the assigned tasks as noted above. It uses *LocalTaskService* API to get the tasks owned by a particular user. We are interested only in tasks that are reserved for this user.

Now we have an EJB to interact with the jBPM engine and return tasks assigned to a user. This will be invoked when a reviewer from Bloom Real Estate management tries to look at the tasks assigned to him or her. So there has to be a user interface for the reviewer to give the command *show my tasks*, a controller component that can take the request and invoke the *TaskFacade* EJB to get the tasks, and finally another user interface to display the task list. Let's build these three components now.

- Create a view page called *admin.jsp* at *WEB-INF/views* as shown below to provide an option to choose role/user ID, which can be for either a reviewer or a superuser. For the human task we are currently working on, the required role is reviewer. In chapter 6 we will be working on a second human task that requires a role of superuser.

```
<%@page contentType="text/html" pageEncoding="UTF-8"%>
<!DOCTYPE HTML PUBLIC "-//W3C//DTD HTML 4.01 Transitional//EN"
        "http://www.w3.org/TR/html4/loose.dtd">
<html>
    <head>
        <meta http-equiv="Content-Type" content="text/html;
        charset=UTF-8">
        <title>Bloom Apartments-Admin</title>
        <link rel="stylesheet" type="text/css"
            href="${pageContext.request.contextPath}/css/style.css"/>
    </head>
    <body>
        <h2>Bloom Rental Application - Admin</h2>
        <hr/>
        <form action="submitadmin" method="POST">
        <table>
            <tr><td>Select your role:</td>
                <td> </td>
                <td><select name="role">
                <option>Reviewer</option>
                <option>Super</option></select></td></tr>
            <tr><td colspan="2"><input type="SUBMIT"
                value="Submit"/></td></tr>
        </table>
        </form>
        <hr/>
    </body>
</html>
```

- Create a POJO called *com.bb.bloomrentalweb.processor.AdminProcessor* to lookup *TaskFacade* EJB. Define a method called *getTasksForReviewer()* as shown below. It simply calls up the EJB, gets a list of *RentalTaskData*, and puts it in as an HTTP request attribute.

```
package com.bb.bloomrentalweb.processor;

import java.util.List;
import javax.naming.Context;
import javax.naming.InitialContext;
import javax.servlet.http.HttpServletRequest;
import com.bb.bloomrentaldomain.RentalTaskData;
import com.bb.bloomrentalejb.task.TaskFacadeLocal;

public class AdminProcessor {

  public void getTasksForReviewer(HttpServletRequest request)
  {
    try {
      Context context = new InitialContext();
      TaskFacadeLocal taskFacade = (TaskFacadeLocal)
                      context.lookup("java:module/TaskFacade");
      List<RentalTaskData> list =
             taskFacade.getAssignedTasks("Reviewer");
      request.setAttribute("rentalTaskDataList", list);
      } catch (Exception e) {
        e.printStackTrace();
      }
    }
  }
}
```

- The *admin.jsp* created above is the first point of entry for Bloom Real Estate management. We need to provide a facility for them to access this page from the URL http://localhost:8080/bloom-rental/showadmin. For that, create a servlet called *com. bb.bloomrentalweb.controller.AdminServlet* and configure it to handle a *showAdmin* request. Ideally, access to this URL should be authenticated and authorized, which we are not doing it here, in keeping with the principle of focusing on only jBPM and closely related activities. Equip *AdminServlet* also to handle the request submitted by the reviewer to display the tasks. The responsibility of reading parameters from the HTTP request and invoking the EJB is delegated to a class called *AdminProcessor*, as can be seen in the code below.

```
package com.bb.bloomrentalweb.controller;

import java.io.IOException;
import javax.servlet.RequestDispatcher;
import javax.servlet.ServletException;
import javax.servlet.annotation.WebServlet;
import javax.servlet.http.HttpServlet;
import javax.servlet.http.HttpServletRequest;
import javax.servlet.http.HttpServletResponse;
import com.bb.bloomrentalweb.processor.AdminProcessor;
    @WebServlet(name="/AdminServlet", urlPatterns= {"/showadmin", "/
    submitadmin"})
    public class AdminServlet extends HttpServlet {
      protected void doGet(HttpServletRequest request,
      HttpServletResponse
            response) throws ServletException, IOException {
        this.doPost(request, response);
      }

      protected void doPost(HttpServletRequest request,
      HttpServletResponse
          response) throws ServletException, IOException {
          if (request.getRequestURI().contains("showadmin")) {
          showAdmin(request, response);
          } else if (request.getRequestURI().contains("submitadmin"))
          {
          submitAdmin(request, response);
          }
      }

      public void showAdmin(HttpServletRequest request,
      HttpServletResponse
          response) throws ServletException, IOException {
          RequestDispatcher disp= request.getRequestDispatcher("WEB-
          INF/views/admin.jsp");
          disp.forward(request, response);
      }

      public void submitAdmin(HttpServletRequest request,
```

```
    HttpServletResponse response) throws ServletException,
    IOException {
   AdminProcessor proc = new AdminProcessor();
   proc.getTasksForReviewer(request);
   RequestDispatcher disp= request.getRequestDispatcher("WEB-INF/
   views/reviewTask.jsp");
   disp.forward(request, response);
 }
 }
```

- Create another view page called *reviewTask.jsp* to display the tasks list. This JSP loops through the task list to display the details of each task, providing an option to approve or reject it. The form in this JSP submits an action of *completeTask* and uses two buttons: *Approve* and *Reject*.

```
<%@page contentType="text/html" pageEncoding="UTF-8"%>
<!DOCTYPE HTML PUBLIC "-//W3C//DTD HTML 4.01 Transitional//EN"
    "http://www.w3.org/TR/html4/loose.dtd">
<%@ page isELIgnored ="false" %>
<%@ taglib uri="http://java.sun.com/jsp/jstl/core" prefix="c" %>
<html>
    <head>
     <meta http-equiv="Content-Type" content="text/html;
     charset=UTF-8">
     <title>Bloom Apartments-Review Task</title>
     <link rel="stylesheet" type="text/css" href="${pageContext.re-
     quest.contextPath}/css/style.css"/>
    </head>
    <body>
    <h2>Bloom Rental Application-Review Task</h2>
```

```
    <hr class="hr50"/>
    <c:forEach items="${rentalTaskDataList}" var="item"
    varStatus="counter">
    <form action="completetask" method="POST">
      <table>
        <tr><td>Task Id:<span/>
        <b><input class="readonlyinput" name="taskId" type="text"
          value="${item.taskId}" readonly/></b></td>
        <td>Task Name:<span/>
      <b>${item.taskName}</b></td>
      <td>Approved By Rules:<span/>
      <b>${item.app.approvedByRules}</b></td></tr>
      <tr><td colspan="3"><h4>Applicant Details:</h4></td></tr>
      <tr><td>First Name:<span/>
      <b>${item.app.firstName}</b></td>
      <td>Task Name:<span/>
      <b>${item.app.lastName}</b></td>
      <td>SSN:<span/>
      <b>${item.app.ssn}</b></td></tr>
    <tr><td colspan="3">Credit Score:<span/>
      <b>${item.app.creditScore}</b></td></tr>
      <tr><td colspan="3" valign="middle">Comments:<span/>
      <textarea rows="4" cols="50" name="comments">Add your com-
    ments here</textarea></td></tr>
      <tr><td><input type="SUBMIT" name="approve" value="Approve"/></
    td>
            <td><input type="SUBMIT" name="reject"
            value="Reject"/></td>
            <td> </td></tr>
      <tr><td colspan="3"><hr/></td></tr>
    </table>
    </form>
  </c:forEach>
  <c:if test="${empty rentalTaskDataList}">
    <h3>No Tasks Available to work on. Have Fun...</h3></c:if>
  <hr class="hr50"/>
  </body>
</html>
```

5.3.2. Completing the Task

We have accomplished a number of things in the last section, including

- Starting and stopping the task server

- Creating a task

- Showing the user a dropdown so that he or she may select the correct user ID

- Showing the tasks assigned to the selected user

The last piece of the puzzle is the step of completing the task. *ReviewTask.jsp* shows user the tasks assigned with the associated data and two buttons—*Approve* and *Reject*—with a text area to include comments. The reviewer can look at the application data and decide to accept the rule engine's decision or to override it. In the real world, the reviewer can base his or her decision on a number of factors. Ideally the application questionnaire should be more elaborate than what we currently have and can include several questions to collect appropriate information about the applicant like annual income, disposable income, number of dependents, whether there are pets, and whether the applicant has references. Then the *Drools Rules* can be enhanced further to provide a decision based on all this information and the reviewer can look at these data to make a determination as to whether or not to accept the rule engine's decision. For the sake of simplicity, we have collected only limited information and laid out a framework for the application, providing a user interface for the reviewer to accept or override the rule engine's decision.

- Add a method called *completeTask()* in the *TaskFacadeLocal* interface with the signature indicated below. It takes three arguments: the identification of the task to be completed, a decision to indicate its approval status, and any comments the reviewer provides while approving or rejecting a rental application.

```
public void completeTask(long taskId, boolean taskApproved, String
taskComments);
```

- Implement the *completeTask()* method in *TaskFacade* as shown below. It uses jBPM API to get a task entity and *inAdmin*, the input parameter of the task. The approval status and comments are set to the input parameter and copied to *outAdmin*, the output of the task. Using Task Service API, the task is started and completed.

```
public void completeTask(long taskId, boolean taskApproved, String
taskComments) {
StatefulKnowledgeSession ksession = null;
long processInstanceId = 0;
    try {
    LocalTaskService service = HumanTaskHelper.getLocalTaskService();
    Task task = service.getTask(taskId);
    processInstanceId = task.getTaskData().getProcessInstanceId();
    ksession = sessionFacade.loadSession(KnowledgebaseBuilder.kbase,
    task.getTaskData().getProcessSessionId());
    Content content = service.getContent(task.getTaskData().
    getDocumentContentId());
    Map<String, Object> contentData = (Map<String, Object>)
    ContentMarshallerHelper.unmarshall(content.getContent(), null);
    RentalAdmin admin = (RentalAdmin) contentData.get("inAdmin");
    admin.setApprovedByreviewer(taskApproved);
    admin.setReviewerComments(taskComments);
    Map<String, Object> results = new HashMap<String, Object>();
    results.put("outAdmin", admin);
    service.start(taskId, "Reviewer");
    service.completeWithResults(taskId, "Reviewer", results);
    } catch (Exception e) {
    e.printStackTrace();
    } finally {
    if (isProcessCompleted(ksession, processInstanceId)) {
      ksession.dispose();
      }
    }
    }
```

```
    private boolean isProcessCompleted(StatefulKnowledgeSession
    ksession, long processInstanceId) {
        ProcessInstance pi = ((org.drools.runtime.process.
        ProcessRuntime)ksession).
                    getProcessInstance(processInstanceId);
        return (pi == null) || (pi != null && pi.getState() ==
        ProcessInstance.STATE_COMPLETED);
    }
```

- After completing the task, the code above checks to see if the process is completed; if so it disposes of the session. As explained earlier, session removal should be attempted after completing a task.

- Add a method called *completeTask()* in the *AdminProcessor* as shown below to retrieve HTTP request parameters, look up *TaskFacade* EJB and call it up.

```
  public void completeTask(HttpServletRequest request)
  {
      try {
String taskIdStr = request.getParameter("taskId");
          String comments = request.getParameter("comments");
          String approve = request.getParameter("approve");
          boolean approved = (approve != null);
          Context context = new InitialContext();
          TaskFacadeLocal taskFacade = (TaskFacadeLocal)
              context.lookup("java:module/TaskFacade");
          taskFacade.completeTask(Long.valueOf(taskIdStr), approved,
          comments);
      } catch (Exception e) {
          e.printStackTrace();
      }
  }
```

- With the back end being ready to complete the task, equip the *AdminServlet* to handle the complete task request from the front end. The code below shows the changes in boldface in the *AdminServlet*.

```java
@WebServlet(name="/AdminServlet", urlPatterns= {"/showadmin", "/sub-
mitadmin", "/completetask"})
public class AdminServlet extends HttpServlet {
    ....
    protected void doPost(HttpServletRequest request,
    HttpServletResponse response) throws ServletException, IOException
    {
            if (request.getRequestURI().contains("showadmin")) {
                showAdmin(request, response);
            } else if (request.getRequestURI().contains("submitadmin"))
            {
                submitAdmin(request, response);
            } else if (request.getRequestURI().contains("completetask"))
            {
                completeTask(request, response);
            }
    }
    ....
    public void completeTask(HttpServletRequest request,
    HttpServletResponse response) throws ServletException, IOException
    {
            AdminProcessor proc = new AdminProcessor();
            proc.completeTask(request);
            RequestDispatcher disp= request.getRequestDispatcher("WEB-
            INF/views/reviewTask.jsp");
            disp.forward(request, response);
    }
}
```

5.4. Running the Application

We have now all the pieces needed to create and complete a human task.

- Copy the BPMN2 XML from the designer and paste it into *com.bb.bloomrentalapp. bpmn2* file in the application.

- Do an mvn clean install, deploy, and start the server. While deploying the *bloom-rental-ear* file, hibernate would update the database schema based on entries in *persistence.xml*.

5.4.1. Preparing the Database

Before moving forward with running the application, there are a few things to be taken care of in the database.

- If you are assigning a task to somebody, that person's user ID should exist in the database table called *Organizational Entity*. You will have to run an SQL in the database as follows:

```
insert into OrganizationalEntity values('User', 'Reviewer');
```

- There should also be an entry in this table for the user named *Administrator*. So run the below SQL too.

```
insert into OrganizationalEntity values('User', 'Administrator');
```

Applications can get the user's data in the database in different ways including inserting the records just before assigning the task to that user or during application start-up or inserting them directly in the database as we just did.

ALERT:

jBPM API provides a very convenient method by means of an interface called *UserGroupCallback* to automatically insert a user into the database just before assigning a task to that user.

- *UserGroupCallback* defines a method called *existsUser(String userId)* to say whether or not the given user exists in a system of record.

- There are four different implementations of *UserGroupCallback* – each uses a different repository for users including Database (*DBUserGroupCallbackImpl*) and LDAP (*LDAPUserGroupCallbackImpl*).

- *UserGroupCallbackManager* helps to register a particular implementation of *UserGroupCallback* with the task engine.

Before assigning a task to a user, if the task engine sees that a *UserGroupCallback* is registered, it calls its *existsUser()* method and inserts the user into the database it the user does not exist.

Since we are using MySQL as our database, run the following commands as well. This is needed because jBPM implementation uses Sequence table to auto-generate ID values; since MySQL does not support Sequence table, we will have to substitute the auto_increment feature.

```
alter table I18NText modify column id bigint(20) auto_increment;
alter table Content modify column id bigint(20) auto_increment;
alter table Task modify column id bigint(20) auto_increment;
```

NOTE: The above "alter table Task" statement fails in *MySQL version 5.6.14* because of RI constraints with other tables, but works fine in version 5.5.34 because of its possible leniency. Therefore *MySQL 5.5.34* is recommended to keep effort to a minimum.

Now the application is ready to test.

- Go to http://localhost:8080/bloom-rental/showapp and submit the application form. You should not see any error in the console/log file. Go to the database and query the task table; you should see a row there with a task assigned to a reviewer and in *Reserved* status.

- Pretend you are the management, and go to http://localhost:8080/bloom-rental/showadmin; select the *Reviewer* option and submit.

- Now you will see a page with the task just created with all the rental application details. Enter some comments and either approve or reject the task; the task should complete just fine. Check the console/log file; it should show the log statements from *LetterDispatchService* and the task table should show that the task is completed.

Summary

Setting up and running a human task could become a difficult if some of the steps herein have not been followed. This chapter addresses all the essential steps to get it up and running. You can significantly improve your understanding of the human task by looking at the jBPM source code and trying to make sense of it. This will also help to diagnose and troubleshoot any problems encountered during usage.

CHAPTER 6

THE BLOOM RENTAL APPLICATION: ADDING GATEWAYS AND A SECOND HUMAN TASK

Next we want to tweak the process flow in such a way that if the reviewer has overridden the decision of the rule engine, we want to get it further reviewed by a superuser and accept or deny the reviewer's decision, as shown below. In BPM, such binary decisions are made by gateways. When you want to take exclusively one path from a gateway, you will use an XOR gateway. After path-specific nodes are executed, both the paths join back at a converging gateway, from which they follow the same path until they encounter the next gateway or the end event.

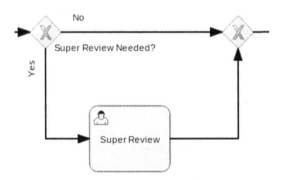

Figure 49. Diverging and converging a gateway.

6.1. Designing the Gateways and the Human Task

- Open the *bloom-rental* business process diagram in the designer.

- Remove the connection between the **Manual Review** user task and the **LetterDispatchService** by selecting the connecting object between the two tasks and deleting it. Move the **LetterDispatchService** and end event to the far right, to make room for additional nodes in between.

- Select **Manual Review** and choose the Data based Exclusive (XOR) Gateway option from the context-sensitive palette. An XOR gateway allows the definition of multiple paths emanating from it, but only one gets executed during runtime. Each path will have a condition associated with it; whichever condition satisfying the runtime context will get executed. Name the gateway *Super Review Needed?*.

Figure 50. Super Review Needed? XOR gateway.

- Multiple paths emanating from a gateway have to converge in another gateway. In our case the first path is a do-nothing pathway since the reviewer has accepted the decision of the rule engine. Let's draw that path first. Select the **Super Review Needed** gateway and choose another XOR gateway from the palette to connect to it. Name this gateway *Super Review Completed*.

- The condition expression corresponding to a path is defined in the path/sequence flow. Select the sequence flow connecting the two gateways and define the following properties.

  ○ **Name**: No.

  ○ **Condition Expression Language**: java.

  ○ **Probability**: 50.0 (Since there are two paths from the gateway, by setting it to 50.0, we are saying that each has an equal probability of making it. The sum of the probabilities of all gateways should be 100).

  ○ **Condition Expression**:

    return (admin.isApprovedByreviewer() == app.isApprovedByRules());

Figure 51. The properties of the first gateway path.

- To define the second possible path from the *Super Review Needed* gateway, select that, choose the task icon from the palette, and bring it downward. Mark it as a user task. Select the sequence flow connecting to the user task, and define the following properties.

    ○ **Name**: Yes.

    ○ **Condition Expression Language**: java.

    ○ **Probability**: 50.0.

    ○ **Condition Expression**:

    return (admin.isApprovedByreviewer() != app.isApprovedByRules());

- Now the new user task needs to be connected to the converging gateway. To do that, open the left-side pane in the designer by clicking the >> symbol in the top left corner. Expand **Connecting Objects**, select **Sequence Flow**, and drag and drop it onto the canvas near the user task. Pull the sequence flow's left edge and drop it into the center of the user task. Similarly, pull the sequence flow's right edge and drop it into the center of the converging gateway.

- Connect the converging gateway to the **LetterDispatchService** in a similar fashion.

- Define the user task as follows:

    ○ **Name**: Super Review Task.

    ○ **Actors**: #{admin.superUserid}.

    ○ **TaskName**: Super Review Task.

    ○ This user task takes the same input and output as the first user task. The data input set is shown below.

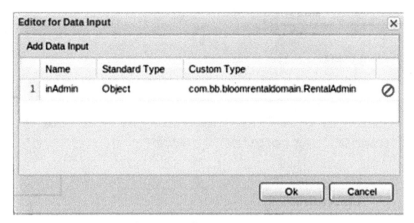

Figure 52. The data input for the super review human task.

○   The data output set is shown below.

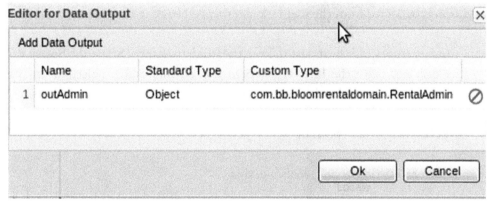

Figure 53. The data output for the super review human task.

○   The data assignments are shown below.

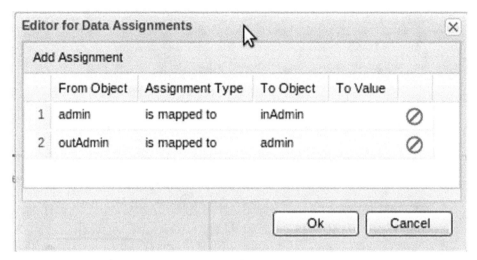

Figure 54. The data assignments for the super review human task.

We are keeping this user task much similar to the *Manual Review* user task, where a variable *inAdmin* is mapped from the process variable *admin* and injected into the user task and a variable *outAdmin* is outjected from the user task and mapped back to the process variable admin.

- Create an empty task form just to keep the validator happy. Select the **Super Review** user task and select the **Edit Task Form** icon on the context palette to enter into a form editor. Just save it with no contents.

- Save the process and check in.

In the end, the process flow should look like this:

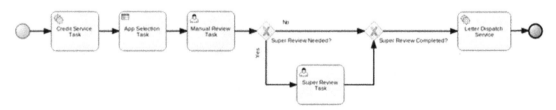

Figure 55. The business rental process with all nodes.

6.2. Updating the Application Code

- Update *com.bb.bloomrentaldomain.RentalTaskData* to have *RentalAdmin* as a member variable to report the decision and the comments made by the reviewer. Also add a getter and a setter for this variable.

```
private RentalAdmin admin;
```

- Just as for the first human task, update *com.bb.bloomrentaldomain.RentalAdmin* to add three variables: *superUserid*, *approvedBySuper*, and *superComments* with getters and setters. Not surprisingly, the first one is the user ID of the person reviewing the second human task, the second variable says whether or not the person approved it, and the last variable captures the comments made by that person.

```
private String superUserid;
private boolean approvedBySuper;
private String superComments;
```

- Update *LetterDispatchService* to log the messages to show the comments from both the reviewer and superuser as shown below.

```
package com.bb.bloomrentalejb.external;

import org.slf4j.Logger;
import org.slf4j.LoggerFactory;

import com.bb.bloomrentaldomain.RentalAdmin;

public class LetterDispatchService {
        private static Logger log = LoggerFactory.
        getLogger(LetterDispatchService.class);

        public void sendLetter(Object param) {
            log.info("Calling from LetterDispatchService...");

            RentalAdmin admin = (RentalAdmin)param;

            log.info("The reviewer has "+ (admin.isApprovedByreviewer()
            ?"approved":"rejected")
            + "the task with the following comments:");
            log.info(admin.getReviewerComments());

            if (admin.getSuperComments() != null) {
                log.info("The Super user has "+ (admin.isApprovedBySupe
                r()?"approved":"rejected")
                + "the task with the following comments:");
                log.info(admin.getSuperComments());
            }
        }
}
```

- Currently *TaskFacade* EJB is coded to handle reviewer tasks only. Now it needs to be modified so that it can handle the tasks of both the reviewer and the superuser. To that end, change the signature of the *completeTask()* method in *TaskFacadeLocal* to take a user ID and *RentalAdmin* as parameters, as shown below.

```
public void completeTask(long taskId, String userId, RentalAdmin
admin);
```

- Change the implementation of the *completeTask()* method accordingly to fetch values from the *RentalAdmin* parameter as shown below.

```
public void completeTask(long taskId, String userId, RentalAdmin param) {
    StatefulKnowledgeSession ksession = null;
    long processInstanceId = 0;
    try {
     LocalTaskService service = HumanTaskHelper.getLocalTaskService();
     Task task = service.getTask(taskId);
     processInstanceId = task.getTaskData().getProcessInstanceId();
     ksession = sessionFacade.loadSession(KnowledgebaseBuilder.kbase,
     task.getTaskData().getProcessSessionId());
     Content content = service.getContent(task.getTaskData().
     getDocumentContentId());
     Map<String, Object> contentData = (Map<String, Object>)
     ContentMarshallerHelper.unmarshall(content.getContent(), null);
     RentalAdmin admin = (RentalAdmin) contentData.get("inAdmin");
     if (userId.equals("Reviewer")) {
       admin.setApprovedByreviewer(param.isApprovedByreviewer());
       admin.setReviewerComments(param.getReviewerComments());
     } else if (userId.equals("Super")) {
       admin.setApprovedBySuper(param.isApprovedBySuper());
       admin.setSuperComments(param.getSuperComments());
     }
     Map<String, Object> results = new HashMap<String, Object>();
     results.put("outAdmin", admin);
     service.start(taskId, userId);
     service.completeWithResults(taskId, userId, results);
} catch (Exception e) {
            log.error("Exception in getting completing task", e);
        } finally {
            if (isProcessCompleted(ksession, processInstanceId)) {
                ksession.dispose();
            }
        }
}
```

• Modify *getAssignedTasks()* method in *TaskFacade* to populate the value of the *RentalAdmin* variable for tasks. Also modify the *buildRentalTaskData()* method to take *RentalAdmin* as a parameter.

```
public List<RentalTaskData> getAssignedTasks(String userId) {
    List<RentalTaskData> data = new ArrayList<RentalTaskData>();
    try {
      LocalTaskService service = HumanTaskHelper.getLocalTaskService();
      List<Status> status = new ArrayList<Status>();
      // retrieve only Reserved Tasks
      status.add(Status.Reserved);
      List<TaskSummary> res = service.getTasksOwned(userId, status,
      "en-UK");
      for (Object each : res) {
      TaskSummary t = (TaskSummary) each;
        Task task = service.getTask(t.getId());
        Content content = service.getContent(task.getTaskData()
        .getDocumentContentId());
        Map<String, Object> contentData = (Map<String, Object>)
        ContentMarshallerHelper.unmarshall(content.getContent(), null);
        RentalAdmin admin = (RentalAdmin) contentData.get("inAdmin");
        RentalApp app = (RentalApp) getProcessData(task);
        data.add(buildRentalTaskData(t, app, admin));
      }
    } catch (Exception e) {
      log.error("Exception in getting Assigned Tasks", e);
    }
     return data;
    }

private RentalTaskData buildRentalTaskData(TaskSummary task,
RentalApp app,
      RentalAdmin admin) {
  RentalTaskData data = new RentalTaskData();
```

```
    data.setApp(app);
    data.setAdmin(admin);
    data.setTaskId(task.getId());
    data.setTaskName(task.getName());
    log.info("RentalTaskData:" + data);
    return data;
}
```

- *AdminProcessor* methods are also hardcoded for the reviewer only at present; they need to be generalized. First change the name of the *getTasksForReviewer* () method to *get-Tasks* () and the implementation as shown below.

```
public void getTasks(HttpServletRequest request)
{
    String role = request.getParameter("role");
    request.setAttribute("role", role);
    try {
        Context context = new InitialContext();
        TaskFacadeLocal taskFacade = (TaskFacadeLocal)
        context.lookup("java:module/TaskFacade");
        List<RentalTaskData> list =
                taskFacade.getAssignedTasks(role);
        request.setAttribute("rentalTaskDataList", list);
    } catch (Exception e) {
        log.error("Exception while getting tasks", e);
    }
}
```

- Change the *completeTask*() method of *AdminProcessor* to handle the superuser as shown below.

```java
public void completeTask(HttpServletRequest request)
{
    try {
      String taskIdStr = request.getParameter("taskId");
      String role = request.getParameter("role");
      String approve = request.getParameter("approve");
      boolean approved = (approve != null);
      RentalAdmin admin = new RentalAdmin();
      if (role.equals("Reviewer")) {
        admin.setApprovedByreviewer(approved);
        admin.setReviewerComments(request.
        getParameter("revComments"));
        } else if (role.equals("Super")) {
        admin.setApprovedBySuper(approved);
        admin.setSuperComments(request.getParameter("superComments"));
        }
        Context context = new InitialContext();
        TaskFacadeLocal taskFacade = (TaskFacadeLocal)
        context.lookup("java:module/TaskFacade");
        taskFacade.completeTask(Long.valueOf(taskIdStr), role, admin);
        } catch (Exception e) {
                log.error("Exception while completing task", e);
    }
}
```

- The actor of *Super Review Task* needs to be set, so add the following in *AppProcessor. buildRentalAdmin()* next to where the actor of the *Review Task* is set.

```java
private RentalAdmin buildRentalAdmin()
{
    RentalAdmin admin = new RentalAdmin();
    admin.setReviewUserid("Reviewer");
    admin.setSuperUserid("Super");
    return admin;
}
```

- Modify the *submitAdmin()* method in the *AdminServlet* to call *AdminProcessor.getTasks()* instead of *AdminProcessor.getTasksForReviewer()*.

- There are no changes in the servlet. For the view, the changes are only in *reviewTask. jsp*, since the same JSP will be used to display the superuser tasks and approve or reject them. Make the changes in that file as shown below.

```jsp
<%@page contentType="text/html" pageEncoding="UTF-8"%>
<!DOCTYPE HTML PUBLIC "-//W3C//DTD HTML 4.01 Transitional//EN"
    "http://www.w3.org/TR/html4/loose.dtd">
<%@ page isELIgnored="false"%>
<%@ taglib uri="http://java.sun.com/jsp/jstl/core" prefix="c"%>
<html>
<head>
<meta http-equiv="Content-Type" content="text/html; charset=UTF-8">
<title>Bloom Apartments-Review Task</title>
<link rel="stylesheet" type="text/css"
    href="${pageContext.request.contextPath}/css/style.css" />
</head>
    <table>
    <tr>
    <td>Task Id:<span /> <b><input class="readonlyinput"
    name="taskId" type="text" value="${item.taskId}" readonly /></
    b></td>
    <td>Task Name:<span /> <b>${item.taskName}</b></td>
    <td>Approved By Rules:<span /> <b>${item.app.approvedByRules}</
    b></td>
    </tr>
    <tr><td colspan="3"><h4>Applicant Details:</h4></td></tr>
    <tr><td>First Name:<span /><b>${item.app.firstName}</b></td>
       <td>Task Name:<span /> <b>${item.app.lastName}</b></td>
       <td>SSN:<span /> <b>${item.app.ssn}</b></td></tr>
    <tr><td colspan="3">Credit Score:<span />
     <b>${item.app.creditScore}</b></td></tr>
    <c:if test="${role eq 'Super'}">
     <tr><td colspan="3" valign="middle">Reviewer Comments:<span />
```

```
      <textarea rows="4" cols="50" name="revComments" disabled>
      ${item.admin.reviewerComments}</textarea></td></tr>
       <tr><td colspan="3" valign="middle">Super user Comments:<span
       />
      <textarea rows="4" cols="50" name="superComments">
      ${item.admin.superComments}</textarea></td></tr>
      </c:if>
      <c:if test="${role ne 'Super'}">
       <tr><td colspan="3" valign="middle">Reviewer Comments:<span />
      <textarea rows="4" cols="50" name="revComments">
      ${item.admin.reviewerComments}</textarea></td></tr>
      </c:if>
       <tr>
         <td><input type="SUBMIT" name="approve" value="Approve" /></td>
         <td><input type="SUBMIT" name="reject" value="Reject" /></td>
         <td> </td></tr>
       <tr>
         <td colspan="3"><hr /></td>
       </tr>
       <input name="role" type="hidden" value="${role}" />
      </table>
   </form>
</c:forEach>
<c:if test="${empty rentalTaskDataList}">
<h3>No Tasks Available to work on. Have Fun...</h3>
</c:if>
<hr class="hr50" />
</body>
</html>
```

6.3. Preparing the Database

Create *Super* user in the Organizational Entity database by running the following SQL.

```
insert into OrganizationalEntity values('User', 'Super');
```

6.4 The Final Run

Grab the BPMN2 file from the designer and put it into the application; do an mvn `clean install` and crank up the application.

- Submit an application from http://localhost:8080/bloom-rental/showapp.

- Select your role as *Reviewer* from http://localhost:8080/bloom-rental/showadmin and submit.

- You will see the application submitted in the first step assigned to you (*Reviewer*) as a task.

- Note whether the application has been approved by the rule engine or not.

- Accept the decision of the rule engine: if the decision is true, hit *Approve*; if the decision is false, hit *Reject*.

- Check the log file; you will see the appropriate message from the *LetterDispatchService*.

- Now submit another new application.

- Select your role as *Reviewer* from http://localhost:8080/bloom-rental/showadmin and submit to see a task assigned.

- This time, override the rule engine's decision: if the decision is true, hit *Reject*; if the decision is false, hit *Approve*.

- Now a task should be assigned to the *superuser*. You can see it when you go to http://localhost:8080/bloom-rental/showadmin and submit your role as *Super*.

- Add your comments and approve or reject.

- The log file should reflect the corresponding message from the *LetterDispatchService*.

Summary

In this chapter we took a very simple use case and learned to use very basic yet important features of jBPM. The final business process consists of:

- two service tasks

- a rule task

- two human tasks

- a converging and diverging XOR gateway

Most basic real-world business processes would require only the tools and techniques learned here. But certainly this is not enough to gain mastery in jBPM. However, this first section, "The Basics," has given you a good enough familiarity with the process. Now we will move on to section 2, "Advanced Techniques", which takes a deep dive and looks beyond the surface.

SECTION 2
ADVANCED TECHNIQUES

CHAPTER 7

PREPARING FOR CUSTOMIZATIONS

Section 1 of the book covered some of the out-of-the-box features of jBPM. Though the out-of-the-box features would be sufficient for a majority of cases, jBPM developers have designed the framework in such a way that users can easily extend its features or customize it to their specific needs.

In the remaining chapters of the book, we will wear a different hat and look at some possible avenues where jBPM can be extended. Specifically, we will go through four things:

- Converting the *LetterDispatchService* as a domain process—the custom service task. (Actually, this is a standard feature of jBPM; but for lack of a better place, this chapter is placed in this section.)

- Creating a custom human task server and switching user tasks to this custom server.

- Adding a timer to the flow and integrating it with Quartz.

- Creating some BAM reports with a custom console.

The remaining chapters will continue to use the Bloom rental application business process; however, in order to avoid possible collision and confusion, the version that came in the previous section will be left intact and a new business process will be cloned off that with a different name. A new copy of the application code will be used with a package name of *com. bb.cust* and all projects will use the term *bloom-rental-cust* instead of *bloom-rental*. Further, a new database instance will be used. The instructions below can be used as a checklist to setup the new environment.

- Create a new database called *bloomCustdb* in MySQL.

- Create a new directory, *bloom-cust-workspace*, and another directory under it with the name *bloom-rental-cust*.

- Create pom.xml under *bloom-rental-cust* with the following contents.

```xml
<project xmlns="http://maven.apache.org/POM/4.0.0" xmlns:xsi="http://
www.w3.org/2001/XMLSchema-instance" xsi:schemaLocation="http://maven.
apache.org/POM/4.0.0  http://maven.apache.org/mavenv4_0_0.xsd">
  <modelVersion>4.0.0</modelVersion>
  <groupId>com.bb.cust</groupId>
  <artifactId>bloom-rental-cust</artifactId>
  <packaging>pom</packaging>
  <version>1.0.0</version>
  <name>bloom-rental-cust</name>
<properties>
    <project.build.sourceEncoding>UTF-8</project.build.sourceEncoding>
  </properties>
  <modules>
  </modules>
<build>
  <plugins>
    <plugin>
      <groupId>org.apache.maven.plugins</groupId>
      <artifactId>maven-compiler-plugin</artifactId>
      <version>2.3.2</version>
      <configuration>
        <source>1.6</source>
        <target>1.6</target>
      </configuration>
    </plugin>
  </plugins>
  </build>
</project>
```

- Move to *bloom-rental-cust* in Command Terminal and create *bloom-rental-cust-domain*, *bloom-rental-cust-web*, *bloom-rental-cust-ejb*, and *bloom-rental-cust-ear* projects using the following Maven commands.

```
mvn archetype:generate -DarchetypeArtifactId=maven-archetype-quickstart
-DgroupId=com.bb.cust -DinteractiveMode=false -DartifactId=bloom-rental-
cust-domain
```

```
mvn archetype:generate -DarchetypeGroupId=org.codehaus.mojo.
archetypes -DarchetypeArtifactId=webapp-javaee6 -DinteractiveMode=false
-DgroupId=com.bb.cust -DartifactId=bloom-rental-cust-web
```

```
mvn archetype:generate -DarchetypeGroupId=org.codehaus.mojo.archetypes
-DarchetypeArtifactId=ejb-javaee6 -DinteractiveMode=false -DgroupId=com.
bb.cust -DartifactId=bloom-rental-cust-ejb
```

```
mvn archetype:generate -DarchetypeGroupId=org.codehaus.mojo.archetypes
-DarchetypeArtifactId=ear-javaee6 -DinteractiveMode=false -DgroupId=com.
bb.cust -DartifactId=bloom-rental-cust-ear
```

- Create an Eclipse workspace under *bloom-cust-workspace* directory and import all the Maven projects into it. Beware of the potential errors and warnings, and fix them using the directions from chapter 1.

- Add the following dependencies to *bloom-rental-cust-ear/pom.xml*.

```
<dependencies>
      <dependency>
         <groupId>com.bb.cust</groupId>
         <artifactId>bloom-rental-cust-web</artifactId>
         <version>1.0-SNAPSHOT</version>
         <type>war</type>
      </dependency>
      <dependency>
         <groupId>com.bb.cust</groupId>
         <artifactId>bloom-rental-cust-ejb</artifactId>
         <version>1.0-SNAPSHOT</version>
         <type>ejb</type>
      </dependency>
      <dependency>
         <groupId>com.bb.cust</groupId>
         <artifactId>bloom-rental-cust-domain</artifactId>
         <version>1.0-SNAPSHOT</version>
         <type>jar</type>
      </dependency>
   </dependencies>
```

- Add the <modules> section under the <configuration> section in *bloom-rental-cust-ear/pom.xml.*

```
<modules>
   <webModule>
      <groupId>com.bb.cust</groupId>
      <artifactId>bloom-rental-cust-web</artifactId>
      <bundleFileName>bloom-rental-cust-web-1.0-SNAPSHOT.war</
      bundleFileName>
      <contextRoot>/bloom-rental-cust</contextRoot>
   </webModule>
```

```
    <ejbModule>
        <groupId>com.bb.cust</groupId>
        <artifactId>bloom-rental-cust-ejb</artifactId>
        <bundleFileName>bloom-rental-cust-ejb-1.0-SNAPSHOT.jar</
        bundleFileName>
    </ejbModule>
  </modules>
```

- Add *bloom-rental-cust-domain* as a dependency in both the *bloom-rental-cust-web* and *bloom-rental-cust-ejb* POM files.

```
<dependency>
    <groupId>com.bb.cust</groupId>
    <artifactId>bloom-rental-cust-domain</artifactId>
    <version>1.0-SNAPSHOT</version>
    <type>jar</type>
</dependency>
```

- Add *bloom-rental-cust-ejb* as a dependency in the *bloom-rental-cust-web* POM file. From *bloom-rental-cust* project, **right click->Maven->Update Project->OK**.

```
<dependency>
    <groupId>com.bb.cust</groupId>
    <artifactId>bloom-rental-cust-ejb</artifactId>
    <version>1.0-SNAPSHOT</version>
    <type>jar</type>
</dependency>
```

- Add jBPM dependencies and a property for the jBPM version to *bloom-rental-cust-ejb/pom.xml*, using the instructions from section 1.1.4.

- Add *org.dom4j* dependency in *MANIFEST.MF* at *bloom-rental-cust-ear* and export it.

- Turn off JPA-JSP Validations from the Eclipse preferences.

- Copy the source code from each *bloom-rental* project to the corresponding *bloom-rental-cust* project and rename the packages from *com.bb* to *com.bb.cust* using the refactoring feature in the *Eclipse*. Change the imported classes in each file to reflect the new package structure.

- Copy also the *css* file and *jsp* files to the *bloom-rental-cust-web* project.

- Remember to grab the application.xml from *bloom-rental-ear* and change it as shown below.

```xml
<?xml version="1.0" encoding="UTF-8"?>
<application xmlns="http://java.sun.com/xml/ns/javaee"
        xmlns:xsi="http://www.w3.org/2001/XMLSchema-instance"
        xsi:schemaLocation="http://java.sun.com/xml/ns/javaee http://
        java.sun.com/xml/ns/javaee/application_6.xsd"
        version="6">
    <display-name>bloom-rental-cust-ear</display-name>
    <module>
        <web>
            <web-uri>bloom-rental-cust-web-1.0-SNAPSHOT.war</
            web-uri>
            <context-root>/bloom-rental-cust</context-root>
        </web>
    </module>
    <module>
            <ejb>bloom-rental-cust-ejb-1.0-SNAPSHOT.jar</ejb>
    </module>
    <library-directory>lib</library-directory>
</application>
```

- Create a new datasource called *bloomCustDS* in *standalone.xml* under the JBoss configuration to point to the new database *bloomCustdb*. Restart the JBoss server.

- Modify persistence.xml from *bloom-rental-ejb* to point to the new datasource *bloomCustDS*.

- Copy *app-selection.drl* from *bloom-rental-ejb* project and paste it at *bloom-rental-ejb/src/main/resources*. Change its import statement for the new package name.

- From the *Designer*, create a package *com.bb.cust*. Open the *bloomrentalapp* process from *com.bb* and copy it to the package *com.bb.cust* with the name *bloomcustrentalapp*. Change its name in the properties pane to *bloomcustrentalapp*, the package to *com.bb.cust*, and the ID to *com.bb.cust.bloomcustrentalapp*.

- Change the process variables and task parameters to reflect the new package names in the model classes.

- Generate task forms for user tasks, generate an image for the process, save the changes, and check in.

- Similarly, copy *app-selection.drl* to the new package and change its import statement for the new package name.

- Download the BPMN2 file and copy it into *bloom-rental-cust-ejb/bloom-rental-ejb/src/main/resources*.

- Go to the *com.bb.cust.bloomrentalejb.process.KnowledgebaseBuilder* class and update the BPMN resource name with the new name.

- Go to *com.bb.cust.bloomrentalweb.processor.AppProcessor* and change the ID of the process to reflect the new process ID *com.bb.cust.bloomcustrentalapp* where *processFacade.startProcess()* is called up.

  - Do an `mvn clean install` and deploy the application.

  - Run the insert and alter statements in the database *bloomCustdb* as mentioned in the chapter 5 and chapter 6.

  - Now launch the URL http://localhost:8080/bloom-rental-cust/showapp. All features developed in section 1 should carry over and function as such.

CHAPTER 8

THE DOMAIN-SPECIFIC PROCESS

The whole idea of a domain-specific process is to promote reusability and extensibility: a task is defined once with a specific signature and no associated functionality, which can be used in different business processes, with each using the same or different implementations (handlers). It is akin to creating an interface in an API and letting the consumers of the API define their own implementations. This process can expose one or more parameters and optionally emit an output back into the process context. It is not much different from the service task available out of the box, except in the following ways.

- A service task can have only data input and must be named *Parameter*, whereas a domain-specific process can have any number of parameters, including none.

- A service task data output must be named *Result*, while the name can be anything in a domain-specific task.

- One specifies the interface and operation for a service task in the designer, whereas for a domain-specific process one specifies the service class at the point of usage in the application.

For our exercise, we will be converting the *LetterDispatchService*, the last step in the Bloom rental application, into a domain-specific process.

8.1. Designing a Domain-Specific Process

When a domain-specific process is defined, an icon will appear for it on the left-side palette of the designer canvas, under **Service Task**. By default, there are already two icons under **Service Task**: **Log** and **Email**. Our aim is to get another icon there for *LetterDispatchService* so that it can be simply dragged and dropped.

- First, identify an image/icon to associate with the domain-specific process. For a service dispatching a letter, something like the icon below would be appropriate.

Figure 56. The letter image.

- From the *Guvnor*, **Create New->Create a File**. Name the file *letterimg* and set the file format as *gif*, *jpg*, or *png*, depending on which format the above image is saved in. Make sure the package *com.bb.cust* is selected. Click **OK**. On the next screen, upload the letter image file and save the changes.

Figure 57. Creating a new file for an image.

- Next we will create what is called a *WorkItemDefinition* file, the purpose of which is to store the signatures of domain-specific processes. Again, from the left-side menu, choose **Create New -> New Work Item Definition**. Give it a name and click **OK**.

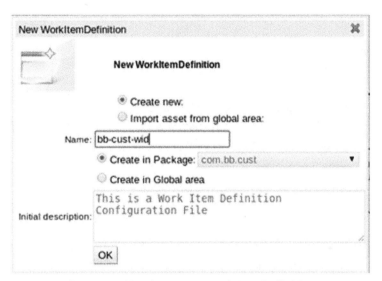

Figure 58. Creating a new WorkItemDefinition.

- Remove the default contents in the WorkItemDefinition editor, enter the following contents and save the changes.

```
import org.drools.process.core.datatype.impl.type.ObjectDataType;
[
    [
        "name" : "LetterDispatchService",
        "parameters" : [
        "param" : new ObjectDataType()
        ],
        "results" : [
                "Result" : new ObjectDataType()
        ],
            "displayName" : "LetterDispatchService",
            "icon" : "http://localhost:8080/drools-guvnor/rest/packages/
            com.bb.cust/assets/letterimg/binary",
        ]
]
```

The above definition declares that a service with the name *LetterDispatchService* takes a parameter *param* of type *Object* and produces an *Object* as output with the name *Result* and uses *letterimg* as its icon. Make sure the value of *icon* above reflects the exact URL of the letter image uploaded.

- Open the *bloomcustrentalapp* business process and expand the **Service Task** option on the left side to see *LetterDispatchService*.

Figure 59. The LetterDispatchService as a domain-specific process.

- Remove the current *LetterDispatchService* node from the Bloom rental business process and drag and drop the new domain process that you see under Service Tasks with the same name. Connect the new *LetterDispatchService* to the *Super Review Completed* gateway and the *End* event. Set its properties as shown below. **DataInputSet** and **DataOutputSet** are already set based on the WorkItemdefinition; in the assignments, map the process variable *admin* to *param*. Ignore the output *Result* variable, since it is not needed in this use case. As can be noticed, we are not specifying the class name and method name as in the case of the regular service task.

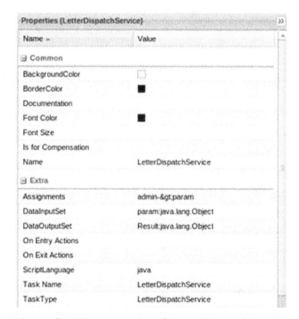

Figure 60. The properties of LetterDispatchService.

- Save the changes and check in.

8.2. Updating the Application Code

Now the jBPM process engine needs to know what code to execute when the process execution encounters a *LetterDispatchService* task node. In other words, we need to write a work item handler and register it for the *LetterDispatchService*. Any work item handler should implement an interface called *org.drools.process.instance.WorkItemHandler* which defines two methods: *executeWorkItem*() and *abortWorkItem*(); the former gets called up at the time of execution of the work item and the latter is usually left with an empty body.

- Go to *com.bb.cust.bloomrentalejb.external.LetterDispatchService* in the *bloom-rental-cust* workspace. Change it to implement *org.drools.process.instance.WorkItemHandler* and define the body of *executeWorkItem* as shown below. Get rid of the *sendLetter*() method.

```
public void executeWorkItem(WorkItem workItem, WorkItemManager man-
ager) {
    log.info("Calling from LetterDispatchService...");
    RentalAdmin admin = (RentalAdmin)workItem.getParameter("param");

    log.info("The reviewer has "+ (admin.isApprovedByreviewer()?"appr
    oved":"rejected") + "the task with the following comments:");
    log.info(admin.getReviewerComments());
    log.info("The Super user has "+ (admin.isApprovedBySuper()?"appro
    ved":"rejected") + "the task with the following comments:");
    log.info(admin.getSuperComments());
    Map<String, Object> results = new HashMap<String, Object>();
    results.put("Result", null); //use this to pass data back to the
    process context
    manager.completeWorkItem(workItem.getId(), results);
}
```

- Register the above work item handler before starting the process in *ProcessFacade. startBPM*() using the following:

```
ksession.getWorkItemManager().registerWorkItemHandler("LetterDispatc
hService",
                                new LetterDispatchService());
```

That's it! Go ahead—copy the BPMN2 file contents from the *Guvnor*, put it into the application, build and run the application at http://localhost:8080/bloom-rental-cust/showapp. It should work seamlessly. This is a very simple example of a domain-specific process, yet it explains how it should be approached and implemented.

CHAPTER 9

THE CUSTOM HUMAN TASK SERVER

At the time of the writing of this book, jBPM offers three different types of implementations for a human task server—Mina, HornetQ, JMS and Local—with each being suitable for certain types of applications. In our example so far, we have used a local human task server. Now we are going to expand on the HornetQ implementation of human task server, to use a Message Driven Bean (MDB) to consume messages.

9.1. The Local Human Task Server

There are two important touch points between a process engine with a human task and a task server, even though jBPM implementations provide several methods in the API to interact with the task server. Let's first see how a local human task server is implemented by looking at the flow of execution in those two significant moments—namely, creating a task and completing a task.

9.1.1 Task Creation

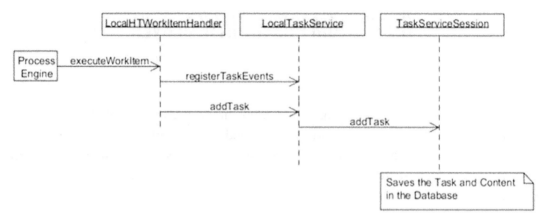

Figure 61. The local task server: task creation.

Before starting a process, the work item handlers are registered for all tasks including human tasks. In the case of the local human task server, the work item handler would be *LocalHTWorkItemHandler*. When the process execution comes to a human task, it calls up the *executeWorkItem* () method of registered handler, which is *LocalHTWorkItemHandler* in this case. This handler, in turn, first registers three response handlers to identify the handler to be called when the task is completed, has failed, or is skipped and then calls up the *addTask* method of the *LocalTaskService*, which in turn calls up the *addTask* from *TaskServiceSession* to create a *Workitem*, a *Task*, and *Content* in the database.

9.1.2. Task Completion

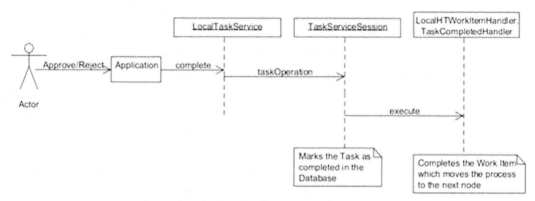

Figure 62. The local task server: task completion.

The task completion cycle uses the same *LocalTaskService* and *TaskServiceSession* classes. When the reviewer or superuser completes a task, the application infrastructure will call up *complete* or *completeWithResults* from the LocalTaskService, which calls up the *taskOperation* method of *TaskServiceSession* in turn to physically mark the task as completed in the database. Now, in order for the process to move to the next step, the work item has to be completed by calling *WorkItemManager.completeWorkItem*. A Local HT server implementation hands over this assignment to the inner class of the *LocalHTWorkItemHandler* called *TaskCompletedHandler*. As has been explained above, while adding the task, this handler was designated to be the one to be called up on task completion, by calling up *registerTaskEvents*. With the call to *completeWorkItem*, the process moves away from the human task.

9.2. The Bloom JMS Human Task Server

As seen above, the local task server implementation is fully synchronous where *LocalTaskService* */LocalHTWorkItemHandler* can be perceived logically as being on the client side and *TaskServiceSession* on the (task) server side. Now, if we were to make the interactions between client and server asynchronous, a middleware component or a transport mechanism would have to be inserted between the client and server to handle the communication between them. jBPM provides three such asynchronous implementations: Mina, HornetQ, and JMS. Of them, Mina uses socket communication and HornetQ relies on messaging with native HornetQ API to produce and consume messages. Even though JMS-based implementation uses JMS API, it does not use a message-driven bean to consume messages.

Our custom implementation provides a little twist by producing messages and consuming them using JMS API and application server provided capabilities. Most important, it does not rely on clients to register for the task completion event handler, which can sometimes be problematic.

The chief custom components used in the custom task server are:

- The *BloomJMSHTClientHandler*. This class extends *BaseClientHandler* and is merely a placeholder; it never gets called up in our implementation.

- The *BloomJMSHTClientConnector*. This implements *TaskClientConnector* and is responsible in dispatching a message to the client.

- The *BloomTaskServiceWrapper*. This extends *SyncTaskServiceWrapper* and overrides its methods. *SyncTaskServiceWrapper* imposes a synchronous behavior wherein it expects a response from the task engine that the requested action has been completed. It waits for a period of time for a response. If no response is received, it throws an exception to the process thread. Bloom JMS implementation relaxes this behavior and does not expect the server to provide a response.

- The *BloomJMSHTWorkItemHandler*. This is the work item handler to be registered for human tasks. It uses all of the three classes above to send messages to the JMS provider.

- The *HumanTaskMessagingBean*. This is the message-driven bean marked to receive messages sent by the Bloom JMS handler.

- The *BloomJMSHTService*. This acts as a pass-through layer to hand over messages to the task engine; it also remembers to call up the *BloomTaskCompletedHandler* upon completion of a task.

- The *BloomTaskCompletedHandler*. This finds the owning session of the task just completed, loads and initializes it, and completes the work item.

- The *BloomTaskSessionWriter*: Here the task server gets an opportunity to respond to the client at the completion of processing the request. In our implementation, no response is made.

- The *BloomTaskServer*. This implements *com.bb.cust.bloomrentalejb.task.TaskServer* and provides methods to *start()* and *stop()* the server. This is pretty much a replica of the *LocalTaskServer* used with the local human task server.

The sequence diagrams below explain the execution sequence of a task creation request and a task completion request. All the components explained above can be seen in action here.

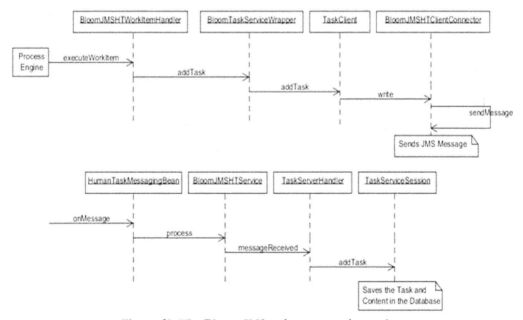

Figure 63. The Bloom JMS task server: task creation.

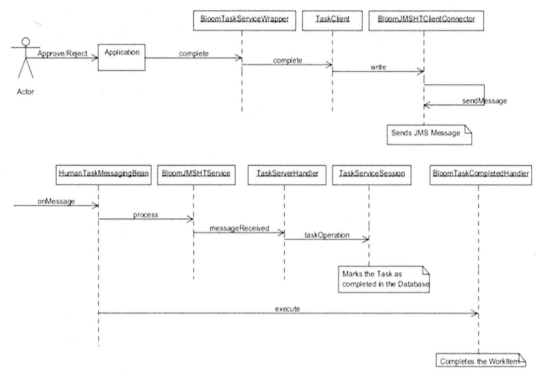

Figure 64. The Bloom JMS task server: task completion.

9.2.1. Implementing a Bloom JMS Human Task Server

- Since the custom JMS server requires messaging services, the JMS option has to be enabled in the JBOSS server. So it has to be started using the configuration in *$JBOSS_HOME/standalone/configuration/standalone-full.xml*. Copy the `<datasource>` and `<driver>` configurations from *standalone.xml* and paste them into *standalone-full. xml*. Now start the server using the option below.

```
$./bin/standalone.sh --server-config=standalone-full.xml

(Use standalone.bat for Windows)
```

- Start the JBOSS command line interface tool by running *$JBOSS_HOME/bin/jboss-cli.sh* or *$JBOSS_HOME/bin/jboss-cli.bat*. Connect to the JBOSS server by entering **connect**. Create the human task queue with the command below and exit the tool.

```
jms-queue add --queue-address=humanTaskQueue --entries=queue/
humanTaskQueue
```

- Copy the following classes from the *ch9* of the source code with this book and paste them into the corresponding locations in your projects.

   - *com.bb.cust.bloomrentalejb.task.HumanTaskMessagingBean*

   - *com.bb.cust.bloomrentalejb.task.TaskServer*

   - *com.bb.cust.bloomrentalejb.task.BloomTaskServer*

   - *com.bb.cust.bloomrentalejb.task.HumanTaskHelper*

   - *com.bb.cust.bloomrentalejb.task.TaskFacade*

   - All the classes under the *com.bb.cust.bloomrentalejb.task.ext* package

- In *com.bb.cust.bloomrentalejb.process.ProcessFacade*, remove the line that registers *LocalWorkItemHandler* and add the following statement.

```
ksession.getWorkItemManager().registerWorkItemHandler("Human Task",

    HumanTaskHelper.getBloomJMSWorkItemHandler(ksession));
```

Now, do an mvn clean install, deploy the target, and run the application. It should create and complete the tasks using the custom JMS server and work seamlessly.

CHAPTER 10

INTRODUCING A DELAY IN THE PROCESS

Often there might be a requirement in business cases where there has to be a delay between two nodes. In the Bloom rental application, we could introduce a delay right after the *App Selection Task* so a task is assigned to the reviewer once every hour or two. For example, a reviewer can expect to get tasks assigned at 10 AM, 12 PM etc., and not anything between 10 AM and 11 AM. If the reviewer is getting notified with an e-mail for each assigned task, frequent e-mails could be annoying, so to batch them all and deliver them every two hours would bring some order into the routine of the reviewer. This could be helpful especially in busy rental seasons like spring or summer. In this chapter, we will look at two different ways to implement such a requirement.

10.1. The Timer Intermediate Event

An ideal candidate for such a scenario would be *Timer Intermediate Event.*

10.1.1. Designing the Timer Intermediate Event

- In *Web Designer*, open the *bloomcustrentalapp* business process and remove the sequence flow between the *App Selection Task* and the *Manual Reviewer Task*. Create ample room between these nodes by moving the *Manual Review Task* and other nodes to the far right.

- Open the shapes palette; drag and drop **Timer Intermediate Event**, circled in the picture below, onto the canvas.

Figure 65. The Timer Intermediate Event.

- Place the Timer event between the *App Selection Task* and the *Manual Reviewer Task* and connect them as shown below.

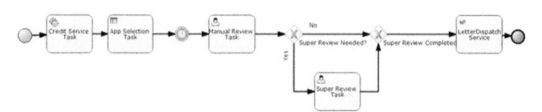

Figure 66. The rental process with Timer.

- Select the **Timer event** and open its Properties pane. Enter its **Name** as *Timer* and set **Timer Duration** as *10s* to indicate that the timer should fire off in ten seconds. Here we are taking a short cut and delaying the process for a fixed ten seconds, though our actual requirement is to assign tasks every two hours.

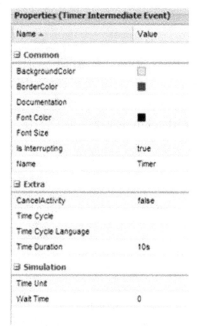

Figure 67. Timer event properties.

- Save the changes and check in.

10.1.2. Running the Application

There is no code change needed in the application. Simply grab the BPMN file and put it in the application workspace. Do an `mvn clean install` and deploy the target. Go to the rental application in the browser and submit the form. You will see the credit score getting reported; the process will then wait for ten seconds before assigning the task.

Though it looks simple enough, there is one big caveat with this solution: the service behind the Timer event is not persistent. If a process is delayed for an hour and if there is a power outage during that time resulting in server restart, the Timer will not fire off at the expiry of the Timer duration and the process will be history. So obviously we need a more robust service that is guaranteed to fire in all situations. Enter Quartz.

10.2. Quartz Integration

Now we will look at a technique to integrate jBPM with Quartz Scheduler to provide a persistent Timer service to a business process that can withstand server restart and outage. In order to demonstrate this technique, the Bloom rental business process will use a Timer service in the same place where the Timer event was used.

10.3. Designing the Timer Service

This is the easy part. All we have to do is define a domain-specific process and drop it into the BPM editor.

- Register a domain-specific process called *BloomTimerService* that takes a parameter called *paramSessionId* to feed the process session ID to the Timer service. Use an image of your choice, name it *timerimg*, and upload it to *Guvnor*. From the designer, add the definition below to the existing WorkItemDefinition file *bb-cust-wid*.

```
import org.drools.process.core.datatype.impl.type.ObjectDataType;
[
  [
    "name" : "LetterDispatchService",
    "parameters" : [
    "param" : new ObjectDataType()
    ],
    "results" : [

      "Result" : new ObjectDataType()
    ],
      "displayName" : "LetterDispatchService",
        "icon" : "http://localhost:8080/drools-guvnor/rest/packages/
        com.bb.cust/assets/letterimg/binary"
    ],

  [
    "name" : "BloomTimerService",
    "parameters" : [
        "paramSessionId" : new ObjectDataType()
      ],
    "displayName" : "BloomTimerService",
    "icon" : "http://localhost:8080/drools-guvnor/rest/packages/com.
    bb.cust/assets/timerimg/binary"
  ]
]
```

- Open the *bloomcustrentalapp* business process and add a process variable called *sessionId* of type String to the process definition.

- Now replace the *Timer* event between *App Selection Task* and *Manual Review User Task* with the *BloomTimerService*. Map the data assignments setting to feed the process variable *sessionId* to *paramSessionId*.

With *BloomTimerService*, the business process should look like this:

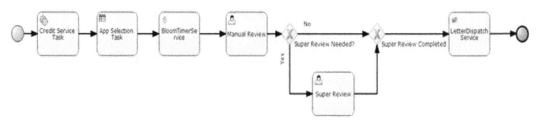

Figure 68. The Bloom rental process with Timer.

10.4. Updating the Application Code

To complete the implementation of Bloom Timer Service from the application side, we will have to create a work item handler and register that handler for *BloomTimerService*. The next question is what the *BloomTimerService* handler will do and how we will integrate it into Quartz. It's actually quite simple: The handler will create a Quartz job to fire at the next scheduled time and end the handler without *completing* the work item. This will persist the session information into the database and halt the further progression of the process. When the Quartz job fires the next morning, it will load the session into memory and complete the work item. That's it, the process will continue from there on. Looks like a hack, doesn't it? It works, nonetheless. Currently we hardcode the *BloomTimerService* to invoke the Quartz job to fire in ten seconds. This can be parameterized to feed the next fire time from the process definition.

This sounds so simple, but there is a small hiccup in this whole setup. In order to schedule jobs, Quartz uses worker (user) threads, and this does not go well in the application server environment. The spawned use-r thread will not have direct access to container resources like JNDI context. For example, from a Quartz job, you cannot look up *UserTransaction* with the default JNDI address of *java:comp/UserTransaction*. jBPM implementation uses only this string literal to lookup a JTA transaction. Second, you cannot lookup an EJB with something like *java:module/TaskFacade.* The Quartz user guide suggests setting a property called *threadsInheritContext.ClassLoaderOfInitializer* to true in *quartz.properties* so that the worker thread will inherit the context of class loader. That doesn't work in JBOSS. So our process must have access to EJBs and *UserTransaction*, and it cannot run in a native worker thread outside of the container scope. How can we overcome this? The suggested work-around below is specific to JBOSS.

JBOSS binds an EJB (for eg., *TaskFacade*) in the EJB JAR in our application at the following JNDI addresses.

1. *java:global/bloom-rental-cust-ear-1.0-SNAPSHOT/bloom-rental-cust-ejb-1.0-SNAPSHOT/ TaskFacade ->.* This is scoped to the application server.

2. *java:app/bloom-rental-cust-ejb-1.0-SNAPSHOT/TaskFacade ->.* This is scoped to the entire application.

3. *java:module/TaskFacade ->.* This is scoped to the EJB module.

When we look up an EJB in a servlet or anywhere in an HTTP request processing cycle, all the above options will work; we usually use the shortest one, which is the *java:module/* option, but from a Quartz thread, the module and app options will not work. Fortunately, however, the *java: global/* option works. This gives an entry point for us to get under the application server umbrella. Once you call up an EJB this way and get inside it, you are a first-class citizen and allowed to use practically all the container resources; so a *java:comp/UserTransaction* and *java:module/EJB* will work just fine. Fair enough? Let's go through the implementation steps.

10.4.1. Setting Up Quartz

- First bundle Quartz with the EAR file by making the following entry in *bloom-rental-cust/pom.xml* under `<dependencies>` and updating the **Maven->Project** from *bloom-rental-cust.*

```
<dependencies>
        <dependency>
                <groupId>org.quartz-scheduler</groupId>
                <artifactId>quartz</artifactId>
                <version>2.2.0</version>
        </dependency>
        <dependency>
                <groupId>org.quartz-scheduler</groupId>
                <artifactId>quartz-jobs</artifactId>
                <version>2.2.0</version>
        </dependency>
</dependencies>
```

- Create *web.xml* in *bloom-rental-cust-web/src/main/webapp/WEB-INF* and initialize Quartz with the following entry in *web.xml*.

```xml
<?xml version="1.0" encoding="UTF-8"?>
<web-app xmlns:xsi="http://www.w3.org/2001/XMLSchema-instance"
xmlns="http://java.sun.com/xml/ns/javaee"
xsi:schemaLocation="http://java.sun.com/xml/ns/javaee http://java.sun.
com/xml/ns/javaee/web-app_3_0.xsd" version="3.0">
    <display-name>bloom-rental-cust-web</display-name>
<context-param>
        <param-name>quartz:shutdown-on-unload</param-name>
        <param-value>true</param-value>
</context-param>
<context-param>
        <param-name>quartz:wait-on-shutdown</param-name>
        <param-value>false</param-value>
</context-param>
<context-param>
        <param-name>quartz:start-scheduler-on-load</param-name>
        <param-value>true</param-value>
</context-param>
<listener>
        <listener-class>
        org.quartz.ee.servlet.QuartzInitializerListener
        </listener-class>
</listener>
</web-app>
```

- Create a file called *quartz.properties* at *bloom-rental-cust-web/src/main/resources* with the following entries.

```
org.quartz.scheduler.instanceName = BloomScheduler
org.quartz.threadPool.threadCount = 3
org.quartz.jobStore.class = org.quartz.simpl.RAMJobStore
org.quartz.scheduler.threadsInheritContextClassLoaderOfInitializer =
true
```

- Add the following system properties in *$JBOSS_HOME/bin/standalone.conf* in Linux or *$JBOSS_HOME/bin/standalone.conf.bat* in Windows.

```
JAVA_OPTS="$JAVA_OPTS -Dorg.quartz.properties=quartz.properties"
For Windows,
set "JAVA_OPTS=%JAVA_OPTS% -Dorg.quartz.properties=quartz.properties"
```

That's it—we are all set with our Quartz configuration.

10.4.2. Creating BloomTimerService

BloomTimerService gets called up when the process hits the Bloom Timer service task; all it does is schedule the Bloom Quartz job to fire at ten seconds from now. But the manner in which we create the job is crucial; it should be created as an EJB and looked up using the *java:global* identifier.

- Create a class called *com.bb.cust.bloomrentalejb.external.BloomTimerService* implementing *org.drools.runtime.process.WorkItemHandler*.

- Implement the *executeWorkItem()* method as shown below.

```
package com.bb.cust.bloomrentalejb.external;

import static org.quartz.JobBuilder.newJob;
import static org.quartz.TriggerBuilder.newTrigger;

import java.util.Calendar;
import java.util.Date;
import java.util.HashMap;
import java.util.Map;

import org.drools.runtime.process.WorkItemHandler;
import org.drools.runtime.process.WorkItem;
import org.drools.runtime.process.WorkItemManager;
import org.quartz.JobDataMap;
import org.quartz.JobDetail;
import org.quartz.Scheduler;
import org.quartz.SchedulerException;
import org.quartz.Trigger;
import org.quartz.impl.StdSchedulerFactory;
import org.quartz.jobs.ee.ejb.EJB3InvokerJob;
import org.slf4j.Logger;
import org.slf4j.LoggerFactory;

public class BloomTimerService implements WorkItemHandler {
    private static Logger log = LoggerFactory.
    getLogger(BloomTimerService.class);

    @SuppressWarnings("rawtypes")
    @Override
    public void executeWorkItem(WorkItem workItem, WorkItemManager
    manager) {
    log.info("Calling from QuartzTimerService...");

       try {

       Integer sessionId = (Integer)workItem.
       getParameter("paramSessionId");
           Scheduler scheduler = new StdSchedulerFactory().
           getScheduler();

           Date currTime = new Date();
```

```
            Map<String, Object> map = new HashMap<String, Object>();
            map.put(EJB3InvokerJob.EJB_JNDI_NAME_KEY,
            "java:global/bloom-rental-cust-ear-1.0-SNAPSHOT/
            bloom-rental-cust-ejb-1.0-SNAPSHOT/BloomQuartzJob");
            map.put(EJB3InvokerJob.EJB_METHOD_KEY, "execute");

            Map<String, Object> argMap = new HashMap<String,
            Object>();
            argMap.put("sessionId", sessionId);
            argMap.put("workItemId", workItem.getId());

            Object[] args = new Object[] { argMap };
            map.put(EJB3InvokerJob.EJB_ARGS_KEY, args);

            Class[] types = new Class[] {Map.class};
            map.put(EJB3InvokerJob.EJB_ARG_TYPES_KEY, types);
            JobDataMap jdmap = new JobDataMap(map);

            JobDetail job = newJob(EJB3InvokerJob.class)
                    .withIdentity("bloom-job-"+ currTime, "bloom-
                    group-"+ currTime)
                    .usingJobData(jdmap)
                    .build();

            Calendar cal= Calendar.getInstance();
            cal.add(Calendar.SECOND, 10);

            Trigger trigger = newTrigger()
                    .withIdentity("bloom-trigger" + currTime, "bloom-
                    group" + currTime)
                    .startAt(cal.getTime())
                    .build();
            scheduler.scheduleJob(job, trigger);

    } catch (SchedulerException e) {
        log.error("Error while scheduling Quartz job", e);
    }
    }
    @Override
    public void abortWorkItem(WorkItem workItem, WorkItemManager
    manager) {}
}
```

Here is what happens in this method:

- ○ Retrieve Quartz scheduler as shown below.

```
Scheduler scheduler = new StdSchedulerFactory().getScheduler();
```

- ○ Since our mission is to call up *BloomQuartzJob.execute()* passing *sessionId* and *workItemId* as arguments in a map, we leverage the *EJB3InvokerJob* provided by Quartz as shown below. Here we tell *EJB3InvokerJob* that EJB to be looked up using the *java:global/* JNDI context and execute method has to be invoked. We also pass in *sessionId* and *workItemId* in a map.

- ○ As with the Timer event, we are taking a shortcut and actually scheduling this job to start ten seconds from now.

```
Calendar cal= Calendar.getInstance();
cal.add(Calendar.SECOND, 10);
//in production, you want to set cal to 9 AM 'tomorrow'
Trigger trigger = newTrigger()
        .withIdentity("bloom-trigger" + currTime,
                 "bloom-group" + currTime)
          .startAt(cal.getTime())
          .build();
scheduler.scheduleJob(job, trigger);
```

- • Register *BloomTimerService* as a *WorkItemHandler* using the statement below before the start of the process as well as after any waiting state; in other words, whenever a knowledge session is being created or loaded. In the business rental process, they are at the following locations.

- ○ *ProcessFacade*

- ○ *BloomTaskCompletedHandler*

- ○ *BloomQuartzJob* (to come in the next section)

```
ksession.getWorkItemManager().registerWorkItemHandler("BloomTimerServi
ce", new BloomTimerService());
```

- The *bloomcustrentalprocess* defines a variable called *sessionId*, which has to be populated before the process starts. Add the below highlighted line in *ProcessFacade.startBPM()* soon after *KnowledgeSession* is created and before the process is started.

```
public void startBPM(String processName, Map<String, Object> pro-
cessData, List<Object> facts) {
UserTransaction ut = null;
StatefulKnowledgeSession ksession = null;
JPAWorkingMemoryDbLogger logger = null;
try {
    Context ctx = new InitialContext();
    ut = (UserTransaction) ctx.lookup("java:comp/UserTransaction");
    ut.begin();
    ksession = sessionFacade.createSession(KnowledgebaseBuilder.
    kbase);
    processData.put("sessionId", ksession.getId());
    ....
    ksession.startProcess(processName, processData);
    ...
}
```

10.4.3. Creating BloomQuartzJob

As said before, the intent of this Quartz job is to load the session and complete the work item. Both session the ID and work item ID come in as parameters. *BloomTimerService* schedules this job to fire. We are working backward here: we implement *BloomTimerService* first and then the Quartz job. Note that, for reasons explained earlier, this job is created as an EJB.

- Create an EJB called *com.bb.cust.bloomrentalejb.external.BloomQuartzJob with a local* interface *com.bb.cust.bloomrentalejb.external.BloomQuartzJobLocal* to define a method with the following signature.

```
public void execute(Map<String, Object> map);
```

- Implement the *execute()* method in *BloomQuartzJob* as shown below.

```
package com.bb.cust.bloomrentalejb.external;

import java.util.Map;
import javax.ejb.EJB;
import javax.ejb.Stateless;
import javax.ejb.TransactionManagement;
import javax.ejb.TransactionManagementType;
import javax.naming.Context;
import javax.naming.InitialContext;
import javax.transaction.UserTransaction;
import org.drools.runtime.StatefulKnowledgeSession;
import org.jbpm.bpmn2.handler.ServiceTaskHandler;
import org.slf4j.Logger;
import org.slf4j.LoggerFactory;
import com.bb.cust.bloomrentalejb.process.KnowledgebaseBuilder;
import com.bb.cust.bloomrentalejb.session.SessionFacadeLocal;
import com.bb.cust.bloomrentalejb.task.HumanTaskHelper;
import com.bb.cust.bloomrentalejb.external.BloomTimerService;

@Stateless
@TransactionManagement(TransactionManagementType.BEAN)
public class BloomQuartzJob implements BloomQuartzJobLocal {
    private static Logger log = LoggerFactory.
    getLogger(BloomQuartzJob.class);

@EJB(lookup="java:module/SessionFacade")
private SessionFacadeLocal sessionFacade;

@Override
public void execute(Map<String, Object> map) {
    UserTransaction ut = null;
    StatefulKnowledgeSession session = null;
        log.info("Executing BloomQuartzJob...");

    try {
        Context ctx = new InitialContext();
        ut = (UserTransaction) ctx.lookup("java:comp/
        UserTransaction");
        ut.begin();
```

```
            int sessionId = (Integer)map.get("sessionId");
            long workItemId = (Long)map.get("workItemId");
            session = prepareSession(sessionId);
            session.getWorkItemManager().completeWorkItem(workItemId,
            null);
        } catch (Exception e) {
            e.printStackTrace();
        } finally {
            try {
                ut.commit();
                session.dispose();
            } catch (Exception e) {
                e.printStackTrace();
            }
        }

    }

}

private StatefulKnowledgeSession prepareSession(int sessionId)
throws Exception {
        StatefulKnowledgeSession ksession = sessionFacade.loadSession(K
        nowledgebaseBuilder.kbase, sessionId);
        ksession.getWorkItemManager().registerWorkItemHandler("Service
        Task",
                new ServiceTaskHandler());
        ksession.getWorkItemManager().registerWorkItemHandler("Human Task",
        HumanTaskHelper.getBloomJMSWorkItemHandler(ksession));
        ksession.getWorkItemManager().registerWorkItemHandler("LetterDi
        spatchService",
        new LetterDispatchService());
ksession.getWorkItemManager().registerWorkItemHandler("BloomTimerSer
vice",
        new BloomTimerService());

        return ksession;
        }
        }
```

The salient things in this implementation here are:

- Retrieving *sessionId* and *workItemId* from the execute method argument map.

- Loading a knowledge session with ID *sessionId* using the *SessionFacadeLocal* EJB and registering work item handlers.

- Completing the work item with ID *workitemId*.

10.4.4. Testing BloomTimerService

Copy the BPMN2 file from designer and put it in the application. Do a Maven build and deploy. Access the application from browser, submit a rental application, and watch the console. In about ten seconds, you should see the Quartz job getting executed and assigning a task to a reviewer.

CHAPTER 11

THE BAM CONSOLE

While jBPM does provide a business activity monitoring (BAM) tool, this chapter goes through creating our own BAM console with minimal features. A BPM console can offer several features, including an ability to

- monitor processes in use

- claim human tasks

- reassign human tasks

- kill a rogue process

- generate various kinds of reports

However, at a basic level, you would expect it to be able to look up processes (both in process and completed), see whether there were any hiccups, and see how the processes performed over time. It gives some visibility inside the processes and provide a means to do a sanity check. This particular feature of BPM tool is a big selling point for adopting BPM, and at some point you may want to use this feature.

It turns out it is extremely straightforward to provide this basic feature in jBPM. There are three tables in the jBPM schema that have auditing information:

- **ProcessInstanceLog** keeps track of the start and end date of each process.

- **NodeInstanceLog** maintains the start and end times of each node of processes, which gives us a good chance to measure the performance and identify the bottlenecks.

- **VariableInstanceLog** stores the process-level variables.

jBPM does not enable auditing by default and it requires instantiating a class called *JPAWorkingMemoryDbLogger* for a knowledge session. The general usage principle is to bind a logger instance of type *JPAWorkingMemoryDbLogger* to the knowledge session whenever it is created or loaded, and to dispose of it once the process completes or hits a waiting state. That is all it takes for the process engine to start writing to the audit tables.

11.1. The BAM Console in the Bloom Rental Application

As noted before, it is incredibly easy to create a simple console. All we need is a UI page to collect a search criteria to narrow down which processes are of interest, a DAO/EJB to pull data from the audit tables, and a second UI page to display the information.

- Create a *JPAWorkingMemoryDbLogger* instance using *ksession* and dispose of it after committing the transaction. The code snippet below shows the steps for *ProcessFacade*.

```java
public void startBPM(String processName, Map<String, Object> pro-
cessData, List<Object> facts) {
    UserTransaction ut = null;
    ProcessInstance processInstance = null;
    StatefulKnowledgeSession ksession = null;
    JPAWorkingMemoryDbLogger logger = null;
    try {
        Context ctx = new InitialContext();
        ut = (UserTransaction)
            ctx.lookup("java:comp/UserTransaction");
        ut.begin();
        ksession = sessionFacade.createSession(KnowledgebaseBuilder.
        kbase);
        processData.put("sessionId", ksession.getId());
        logger = new JPAWorkingMemoryDbLogger(ksession);
        .....
    } catch (Exception e) {
        e.printStackTrace();
        ......
    } finally {
        try {
            ....
            logger.dispose();
        } catch (Exception e) {
            e.printStackTrace();
        }
    }
}
```

- In the same fashion, attach a *JPAWorkingMemoryDbLogger* instance at *com.bb.cust. bloomrentalejb.task.ext.BloomTaskCompletedHandler* and *com.bb.cust.bloomrentalejb.external.BloomQuartzJob* since, at both the places, the rental process resumes from a waiting state.

- Create a POJO *com.bb.cust.bloomrentaldomain.NodeAuditDetail* with the following member variables and add getters and setters. This keeps the start date and end date of each node in the process.

```
private String nodeName;
private int nodeInstanceId;
private Date startDate;
private Date endDate;
```

- Create another POJO *com.bb.cust.bloomrentaldomain.ProcessAuditDetail* with the following member variables and add getters and setters.

```
private String processName;
private long processInstanceId;
private Date startDate;
private Date endDate;
private List<NodeAuditDetail> nodeAuditDetail;
private RentalApp app;
```

The two classes above are used to collect the search criteria and return the results. For starters, we are using only a process name, a start date, and an end date as possible search criteria.

- Create an EJB *com.bb.cust.bloomrentalejb.console.ConsoleFacade* with a local interface *com. bb.cust.bloomrentalejb.console.ConsoleFacadeLocal* to lookup audit tables based on search criteria. Define the below two methods in *ConsoleFacadeLocal*.

```
package com.bb.cust.bloomrentalejb.console;
import java.util.List;
import javax.ejb.Local;
import com.bb.cust.bloomrentaldomain.ProcessAuditDetail;
@Local
public interface ConsoleFacadeLocal {
    public List<ProcessAuditDetail> getProcessAuditDetail(ProcessAudi
tDetail criteria);
}
```

- The implementation of this method basically entails reading the tables *ProcessInstanceLog* and *NodeInstanceLog* for any given process. Reading the table *ProcessInstanceLog* is pretty straightforward, whereas reading *NodeInstanceLog* is a bit tricky—it has only one date column and uses two different records to capture the start date and end date of a node, and it differentiates them by means of a discriminator column called *type*. A value of 0 for type indicates the start row and 1 indicates the end row. The code below shows the implementation of a *ConsoleFacade* EJB.

```java
package com.bb.cust.bloomrentalejb.console;
import java.util.ArrayList;
import java.util.Date;
import java.util.List;
import javax.ejb.Stateless;
import javax.persistence.EntityManager;
import javax.persistence.PersistenceContext;
import javax.persistence.Query;
import org.jbpm.process.audit.ProcessInstanceLog;
import com.bb.cust.bloomrentaldomain.NodeAuditDetail;
import com.bb.cust.bloomrentaldomain.ProcessAuditDetail;
@Stateless
public class ConsoleFacade implements ConsoleFacadeLocal {
    @PersistenceContext(unitName="jpa.jbpm")
    private EntityManager em;
    @SuppressWarnings("unchecked")
    @Override
    public List<ProcessAuditDetail> getProcessAuditDetail(
                ProcessAuditDetail criteria) {
    List<ProcessAuditDetail> result = new ArrayList<ProcessAuditDeta
    il>();
        String psql = "from ProcessInstanceLog where
        processId=:processName "+" and start_date>=:startDate and
        end_date<=:endDate";
    Query query = em.createQuery(psql);
    query.setParameter("processName", criteria.getProcessName());
    query.setParameter("startDate", criteria.getStartDate());
    query.setParameter("endDate", criteria.getEndDate());
    List<ProcessInstanceLog> list = query.getResultList();
    for(ProcessInstanceLog log:list) {
        ProcessAuditDetail detail = new ProcessAuditDetail();
        detail.setProcessName(log.getProcessId());
        detail.setStartDate(log.getStart());
        detail.setEndDate(log.getEnd());
        detail.setProcessInstanceId(log.getProcessInstanceId());
```

```
        detail.setNodeAuditDetail(getNodeDetail(log.
        getProcessInstanceId()));
                result.add(detail);
            }
            return result;
        }
        @SuppressWarnings("unchecked")
        private List<NodeAuditDetail> getNodeDetail(long processIn-
        stanceId) {
        List<NodeAuditDetail> result = new
        ArrayList<NodeAuditDetail>();
        String psql = "select nodeName, min(log_date), max(log_date)
        from NodeInstanceLog "+ "where processInstanceId= :processIn-
        stanceId "+
            "group by processInstanceId, nodeName order by
            nodeInstanceId";
            Query query = em.createNativeQuery(psql);
            query.setParameter("processInstanceId", processInstanceId);
            List<Object[]> list = query.getResultList();
            for(Object[] log:list) {
        NodeAuditDetail detail = new NodeAuditDetail();
        detail.setNodeName((String) log[0]);
        detail.setStartDate((Date) log[1]);
        detail.setEndDate((Date) log[2]);
        result.add(detail);
        }
    }
    return result;
}
}
```

- Add the following three audit entities under both persistence units in *persistence.xml* so the persistence unit will be aware of the audit entities.

```
<class>org.jbpm.process.audit.ProcessInstanceLog</class>
<class>org.jbpm.process.audit.NodeInstanceLog</class>
<class>org.jbpm.process.audit.VariableInstanceLog</class>
```

- Create a JSP called *console.jsp* at *src/main/webapp/WEB-INF/views* in *bloom-rental-cust-web* project to display the search criteria and the results. The following source code shows a very simple JSP page.

```
<%@page contentType="text/html" pageEncoding="UTF-8"%>
<!DOCTYPE HTML>
<%@ page isELIgnored="false"%>
<%@ taglib uri="http://java.sun.com/jsp/jstl/core" prefix="c"%>
<html>
<head>
<meta http-equiv="Content-Type" content="text/html; charset=UTF-8">
<title>Bloom Apartments Console</title>
<link rel="stylesheet" type="text/css"
    href="${pageContext.request.contextPath}/css/style.css" />
</head>
<body>
  <h2>Bloom Rental BAM Console</h2>
  <hr />
  <form action="showlog" method="POST">
    <table>
    <tr><td>Process Name</td>
            <td><input type="text" name="processName"
            , value= "com.bb.cust.bloomcustrentalapp" /></td>
    </tr>


    <tr><td>Start Date</td>
            <td><input type="datetime-local" name="startDate" /></
            td>
    </tr>
    <tr><td>End Date</td>
            <td><input type="datetime-local" name="endDate" /></td>
    </tr>
    <tr><td colspan="2"><input type="SUBMIT" value="Show Log" /></
    td>
    </tr>
    </table>
    </form>
    <hr />
    <c:if test="${not empty processAuditList}">
      <c:forEach items="${processAuditList}" var="item">
```

```
    <table>
      <tr><td>Process Name:<span /> <b>${item.processName}</b></td>
      <td>Process Instance Id:<span /> <b>${item.processInstanceId}</
      b></td>
    </tr>
      <tr><td>Start Date:<span /> <b>${item.startDate}</b></td>
      <td>End Date:<span /> <b>${item.endDate}</b></td>
      </tr>
    </table>
        <hr class="hr50" /><table>
        <tr><td><b>Node Name</b></td>
          <td><b>Start Date</b></td>
          <td><b>End Date</b></td></tr>
        <c:forEach items="${item.nodeAuditDetail}" var="nodeItem">
        <tr><td>${nodeItem.nodeName}</td>
          <td>${nodeItem.startDate}</td>
          <td>${nodeItem.endDate}</td></tr>
      </c:forEach>
      </table>
      </c:forEach>
</c:if>
</body>
</html>
```

- Create a POJO class *com.bb.bloomrentalweb.processor.ConsoleProcessor* to take requests from the servlet and forward them to the *ConsoleFacade* EJB, as shown below.

```java
package com.bb.cust.bloomrentalweb.processor;
import java.text.DateFormat;
import java.text.SimpleDateFormat;
import java.util.Date;
import java.util.List;
import javax.naming.Context;
import javax.naming.InitialContext;
import javax.servlet.http.HttpServletRequest;
import org.slf4j.Logger;
import org.slf4j.LoggerFactory;
import com.bb.cust.bloomrentaldomain.ProcessAuditDetail;
import com.bb.cust.bloomrentalejb.console.ConsoleFacadeLocal;
    public class ConsoleProcessor {
    private static Logger log = LoggerFactory.
    getLogger(ConsoleProcessor.class);
    public void getLog(HttpServletRequest request)
      {
          String role = request.getParameter("role");
          request.setAttribute("role", role);
          try {
              Context context = new InitialContext();
              ConsoleFacadeLocal consoleFacade = (ConsoleFacadeLocal)
                    context.lookup("java:module/ConsoleFacade");
              ProcessAuditDetail criteria = new ProcessAuditDetail();
              criteria.setProcessName(request.
              getParameter("processName"));
              DateFormat df = new
              SimpleDateFormat("yyyy-MM-dd'T'HH:mm");
              Date stDate = df.parse(request.
              getParameter("startDate"));
              Date endDate = df.parse(request.
              getParameter("endDate"));
              criteria.setStartDate(stDate);
              criteria.setEndDate(endDate);
              List<ProcessAuditDetail> list = consoleFacade.getProces
              sAuditDetail(criteria);
              request.setAttribute("processAuditList", list);
              } catch (Exception e) {
              log.error("Exception while getting tasks", e);
      }
    }
}
```

- Create a servlet *com.bb.bloomrentalweb.controller.ConsoleServlet* as shown below to handle HTTP requests from *console.jsp* and forward them to the processor class.

```
package com.bb.cust.bloomrentalweb.controller;
import java.io.IOException;
import javax.servlet.RequestDispatcher;
import javax.servlet.ServletException;
import javax.servlet.annotation.WebServlet;
import javax.servlet.http.HttpServlet;
import javax.servlet.http.HttpServletRequest;
import javax.servlet.http.HttpServletResponse;
import com.bb.cust.bloomrentalweb.processor.ConsoleProcessor;
/**
 * Servlet implementation class SimpleServlet
 */
@WebServlet(name="/ConsoleServlet", urlPatterns= {"/showconsole", "/
showlog"})
public class ConsoleServlet extends HttpServlet {
    private static final long serialVersionUID = 1L;
    /**
     * @see HttpServlet#doGet(HttpServletRequest request,
     HttpServletResponse response)
     */
    protected void doGet(HttpServletRequest request,
    HttpServletResponse response) throws ServletException,
    IOException {
    this.doPost(request, response);
        }
    /**
     * @see HttpServlet#doPost(HttpServletRequest request,
     HttpServletResponse response)
     */
    protected void doPost(HttpServletRequest request,
    HttpServletResponse response) throws ServletException,
    IOException {
        if (request.getRequestURI().contains("showconsole")) {
```

```
        showConsole(request, response);
        }else if (request.getRequestURI().contains("showlog")) {
        showLog(request, response);
    }
}
public void showConsole(HttpServletRequest request,
HttpServletResponse response) throws ServletException,
IOException {
    RequestDispatcher disp= request.getRequestDispatcher("WEB-INF/
    views/console.jsp");
    disp.forward(request, response);
}
public void showLog(HttpServletRequest request,
HttpServletResponse response) throws ServletException,
IOException {
    ConsoleProcessor proc = new ConsoleProcessor();
    proc.getLog(request);

    showConsole(request, response);
    }
}
```

- Do an mvn clean install from the command line and deploy the target application.

- Submit an application from the link http://localhost:8080/bloom-rental-cust/show-app and review and approve or reject it. Now access the link http://localhost:8080/bloom-rental-cust/showconsole to see the console search page; entering a search date and time pulls up the details of the application process just completed.

11.2. Taking the Console to the Next Level

Before starting to develop a BAM console, the first question that should be asked is, who are the targeted users for the console? If it is information technology support, the out-of-the-box console may be enough. But when it is meant to be for business users, we would want to be able to look up processes not only by start date, end date, or process ID but also based on business parameters that identify a process. For example, in the Bloom rental application, we might want to look up processes based on Social Security number or on a credit score between 550 and 600. We may want to see how many Smiths applied for a rental. If we think this through at a little higher level, we clearly realize the need for a way to correlate each process with one or more business parameters that uniquely identify them.

In the context of the Bloom rental process, this would require a twofold effort.

- First, storing the rental application data in the database before kicking off the business process and identifying a key for application.

- Secondly, storing the process instance ID mapping it with the process identifier.

With these two data sets, processes can be searched based on business parameters.

Summary

The techniques described in this chapter are simply pointers to the directions in which customizations could be headed and how. They cannot be considered production ready yet, and no attempt should be made to deploy them into production as is. In general, open-source products offer a great flexibility in that the source code is available for anyone to look at. With some level of effort, it may be easy enough to tweak them in the desired way. But extreme care must be taken before deploying customizations into production. This includes testing the customized product with all possible test scenarios and monitoring the performance.

ABOUT THE AUTHOR

Venkataganesh Thoppae is an author, speaker, entrepreneur, and technology enthusiast. He has worked on technologies from the legacy ALGOL and COBOL to today's jBPM. In the last three years, he got under the hood of jBPM source code to solve some challenging problems; this helped him to get a solid understanding of the subject.

Born in Madurai, India, Venkat immigrated to the United States in 2001 and currently lives with his loving family in Frederick, Maryland. Being a strong achiever from a young age, Venkat completed his engineering studies at the Coimbatore Institute of Technology and graduated with an MBA from the University of Maryland.

Venkat currently consults with Lockheed Martin and has consulted for major Fortune 500 companies including Wells Fargo, GEICO, and Fannie Mae. As an entrepreneur, he is the cofounder of BrainBloom LLC, which provides consulting and training services and also oversees its Indian operations.

www.ingramcontent.com/pod-product-compliance
Lightning Source LLC
Chambersburg PA
CBHW080411060326

40689CB00019B/4210